Justice and Equity

Justice and Equity

Serge-Christophe Kolm

translated by
Harold F. See

with the assistance of
Denise Killebrew
Chantal Philippon-Daniel
and
Myron Rigsby

The MIT Press
Cambridge, Massachusetts
London, England

© 1997 The Massachusetts Institute of Technology

This work originally appeared in 1971 under the title *Justice et Equité* published by Centre d'Etudes Prospectives et d'Economie Mathématique Appliquées à la Planification, Paris, and was reprinted in 1972 by Editions du Centre National de la Recherche Scientifique, Paris.

© 1971 by Serge-Christophe Kolm

Printed and bound in the United States of America.

Library of Congress Cataloging-in-Publication Data

Kolm, Serge-Christohe
    [Justice et équité. English]
    Justice and equity / Serge-Christophe Kolm ; translated by Harold F. See with the assistance of Denise Killebrew, Chantal Philippon-Daniel, and Myron Rigsby.
        p. cm.
    Includes bibliographical references and index.
    ISBN 0-262-11215-9 (alk. paper)
    1. Distributive justice. 2. social justice. I. Title.
HB251.K6413 1997
172'.2--dc21   97-8111
                                                CIP

Contents

Contents

Translator's Acknowledgment

This translation of *Justice et Equité* originated when my own study of "fairness" led me time and again to this work. The content of *Justice et Equité* was new material. Its foundation, analysis, and development of the principles of "equity" and "practical justice" and of a number of related concepts are the origin of major lines of study in normative economics and scientific social ethics. *Justice et Equité* is a seminal work that should be available in English.

I am deeply grateful to Serge Kolm for permitting me the opportunity to translate *Justice et Equité*. I am even more grateful that the experience has permitted me the opportunity to count him as a friend.

The translation of *Justice et Equité* would not have been possible without the work of Denise Killebrew, Chantal Philippon-Daniel, and Myron Rigsby, and the tireless work and dedication of Patty Lovelady Nelson. Serge Kolm and I express our deep appreciation.

H. F. See

Foreword (1997)

1 Presentation

This book is the translation of *Justice et Equité* published in French in 1971,[1] and reprinted in 1972.[2] The initiative and the realization of this translation, and the preparation of this book, are due to Professor Harold See.[3] I wish to express here both my friendly gratitude, and my admiration for this outstanding performance of a difficult task. The translation is without modification, since what I have to add has been and will be the object of other publications.[4]

---

1. CEPREMAP, Paris. Hence over a quarter of a century ago (this was my tenth published book, and the shortest one). A number of translations in languages other than English (including Japanese and Russian) appeared in the early seventies.

2. CNRS, Paris.

3. The Herbert D. Warner Professor of Law at The University of Alabama School of Law, and Associate Justice of the Alabama Supreme Court.

4. See, in particular, "The Theory of Justice," *Social Choice and Welfare* 13(2) (April 1996): 151-82; "The Economics of Social Sentiments, The Case of Envy," *Japanese Economic Review* 46(1) (March 1995): 63-87, which also includes a survey of the field of the analyses of the principles of Equity or "No-envy" and shows how the properties can actually take the sentiment of envy into account; "The Normative Economics of Unanimity and Equality: Equity, Adequacy and Fundamental Dominance," in *Markets and Welfare* (K. J. Arrow ed., Macmillan, London, 1991): 243-86; "Playing Fair with Fairness," *Journal of Economic Surveys* 10(2) (1996): 199-215; "L'égalité de la liberté," *Recherches Economiques de Louvain* 1 (1994): 81-86; "Super-Equité," *Kyklos* 26(4) (1973): 841-43; "Sur les conséquences économiques des principes de justice et de justice pratique," *Revue D'Economie Politique* 1 (1974): 80-107; *Equal Liberty* (CGPC, 1993). A recent survey of other works in the field of Equity can be found in W.

The main topics of this book are the two basic and complementary principles of justice: equality of liberty, and ideal equality of welfare, happiness or "utility" which is relevant in its second-best form of "first take care of the most miserable." A number of other, related social ethical criteria are also considered (fundamental efficiency and majorities, adequacy, and so on). All these concepts are introduced and analyzed, and their properties, relations, and consequences are derived. Some of my earlier publications had presented the analytical bases of these polar principles, as well as the consequences of the third pure constitutive ideal of distributive justice–the equality of incomes, wealths, or goods–, that is to say the general theory of the comparison and measures of unjust inequalities in quantities.[5] Note that equality in end values of justice is a logically necessary ideal, as will be recalled shortly. Later publications completed or developed the social ethics of liberty, of inequalities, of happiness, and of the intrinsic quality of social and economic relations and behavior.[6]

Thomson, *The Theory of Fairness* (Princeton University Press, Princeton, N. J., 1996).

5. See, in particular, the essay "The Optimal Production of Social Justice" (sections 6 and 7), 1966, International Economic Association Conference on Public Economics, Biarritz, proceedings edited by H. Guitton and J. Margolis, *Economie Publique* (CNRS, Paris, 1968): 109-73, and *Public Economics* (Macmillan, London, 1969): 145-201.

6. A short selection of these publications would include the books *The Liberal Social Contract* (*Le Contrat Social Liberal*) (Presses Universitaires de France, Paris, 1985), *The Good Economy, General Reciprocity* (*La Bonne Economie, La Réciprocité Générale*) (Presses Universitaires

The synthetic and global situation of these ideas as constituting the field of overall social and economic ethics and
justice, and as providing the essentials of the solution of the
problem of defining the social optimum, is provided in my
general presentation of this field and of this solution,
Modern Theories of Justice.[7]

If several persons have identical domains of free choice,
no one prefers any other's choice to her own, since she
could have chosen it. Hence if one person prefers another's situation or allocation to her own, these situations-
allocations cannot result from equal freedom in the sense of
identical domains of free choice. Conversely, if no person
prefers any other's situation-allocation to her own, these
situations-allocations can result from an equality of liberty
(the possible identical domains of choice are those that
contain the persons' situations-allocations and any other
situations-allocations that no person prefers to her own).
Hence, no individual preferring any other's situation or
allocation to her own amounts to equal freedom, and it is
labelled *Equity* for *equal independent (instrumental)
liberty.*[8] Liberties can be of many types, including all

---

de France, Paris, 1984), *Happiness-Freedom* (*Le Bonheur-Liberté*)
(Presses Universitaires de France, Paris, 1982), various developments of
the comparison of inequalities in incomes, in bundles of goods, and in
liberties, and various applications in the theory of public economics.

7. The MIT Press, Cambridge, Mass., 1996.

8. The relation between Equity and envy is presented in "The Economics of Social Sentiments, The Case of Envy," op. cit. (a long tradition
has modeled envy as a negative externality; see, for example, my article

kinds of means of action, rights, powers, etc. The analysis
of Equity occupies the first two of the three parts of this
book.

The second end value of justice is happiness and
phenomena of its family (such as satisfaction, the ambigu-

"The Taxation of Conspicuous Consumption" ("La taxation de la
consommation ostentatoire"), *Revue D'Economie Politique* 1 (1972):
65-79, where this structure is used to determine optimum taxation). The
extension to equal interferring (non-independent) liberties is presented in
Equal Liberty, op. cit. Identical domains of choice still imply Equity if
these domains influence individuals' preferences about allocations, for
instance if individuals have preferences about these domains for reasons
other than their preferences about the allocations they can choose and in
addition to these indirect preferences, or for any of the various psychological reasons that make preferences about the alternatives depend on
the domain of possible choice (the "sour grapes" effect is one such
reason). The criterion of Equity as no individual preferring any other's
allocation to her own, without any mention of equal liberty, has been
introduced in economics by its mention by J. Tinbergen in application to
equitable wages and occupations in *Redelijke Inkomensverdeling* (De
Gulden Pers, Haarlem, 1946, in Dutch), following a suggestion from
Tinbergen's professor, the Dutch physicist Ehrenfest, in 1925. This
previous suggestion by Ehrenfest was pointed out to me by Tinbergen in
1962 at a conference in Paris, when I was presenting my analysis of the
measures of inequality later published as sections 6 and 7 of "The
Optimal Production of Social Justice," op. cit. D. Foley cursorily
suggested this form of the criterion (no consumer prefers any other's
goods to her own) in a casual remark in 1967 ("Resource Allocation in
the Public Sector," *Yale Economic Essays* 7 (1967): 49-58).

ous "welfare,"[9] and most importantly reduction of suffer-ing).[10] This topic of the third and last part of this book is particularly relevant in the social situations where certain persons incur particular physical or mental suffering, notably, as concerns economic justice, because their basic needs are not all satisfied.[11] Then, it is generally unfortu-nately all too easy to identify these persons in need. To give priority to this satisfaction underlies the principle called *practical justice* proposed and analyzed in this book. This principle is a maximin–more exactly, for efficiency, a lexicographic maximin or leximin–in interpersonally comparable "fundamental preferences" (which are *a priori* ordinal preferences or utility).[12] The adjective "practical"

---

9. Uses of the term "welfare" oscillate between consumption goods or disposable income on the one hand, and utility, satisfaction or possibly happiness on the other. What is ambiguous about "welfar" concerns which individual capacities to be satisfied it includes.

10. See my book *Happiness-Freedom* (*Le Bonheur-Liberté*), op. cit.

11. On basic needs, see my book *Socialist Transition* (*La Transition Socialiste*) (Editions du Cerf, Paris, 1977), and also *Men of the Fouta-Toro* (*Les Hommes du Fouta-Toro*) (MAS, Saint-Louis, 1959).

12. See my 1966 essay "The Optimal Production of Social Justice," op. cit., which also considers maximin in goods, income, or wealth. In *A Theory of Justice* (Harvard University Press, Cambridge, Mass., 1971), John Rawls proposed a maximin in "primary goods"—which include income and wealth—, or "difference principle," to be applied in all cases, and which is a proposal very different from practical justice. Rawls does not consider here a concept of preference or utility for a very basic reason. He proposes that justice should always be exclusively concerned with individuals' external means to "pursue their life plans"

is used in its Kantian sense of imposed by the constraints
of reality which may prevent the ideal equality or make it
inefficient.

(the "primary goods"), and so he sees individuals' preferences and
capacities for being satisfied as always irrelevant to the direct definition
of the criteria of justice. The issue of sufficiently defining the fundamental preferences is thus not raised. But a number of other issues are
then raised, which are solved by fundamental preferences and practical
justice. Rawls's maximin is in terms of an index of primary goods
which are income, wealth, power, position, and self-respect or the means
to it. Note that the primary goods do not include leisure, each individual
is in general concerned with others' endowments of primary goods
through social interaction, and the weights of the index cannot represent
a linear approximation of fundamental utility since it would then have to
depend on the individual and on the overall allocation. These weights,
and to begin with the measures of "power," "position," and "self-
respect," have to be defined at any rate. Rawls, however, expresses an
interest in fundamental preferences in "Social Unity and Primary Goods,"
in *Utilitarianism and Beyond* (A. Sen and B. Williams eds., Cambridge
University Press, Cambridge, England, 1982): 159-85. P. Hammond,
in "Equity, Arrow's Conditions and Rawls' Difference Principle,"
Econometrica 44 (1976): 793-804, calls practical justice the difference
principle (names may not matter) and derives it from its axiomatic
assumption "in the small," which requires the interpersonal comparability
of fundamental preferences in the full domain (see also Arrow, 1977,
noted below, and further work of K. Roberts). Presently, many
economists use the name of Rawls for practical justice, but this
constitutes a basic incomprehension of the history of the analysis of
social ethics in the last thirty years. I first learned about the difference
principle when I was presenting practical justice to a visiting American
scholar in Paris (Professor Charles Fried of Harvard Law School) and he
told me: "This seems similar to what Rawls is proposing." For the
various reasons just noted, this remark has only a limited scope.

The first two parts of this book use only the classical, ordinal and non-interpersonally compared, preferences and utility functions. By contrast, the third part uses ordinal interpersonally comparable preferences and utilities, the "fundamental" preferences and utility. It uses them minimally for practical justice, since, commonly, in a large society, maximin suffices for leximin and the same people have the lowest levels both before and after the policy, and then all that is required is to find out the most distressed people, which is all too easy when this criterion is the relevant one. But this part also considers cases where more extensive interpersonal (ordinal) comparisons are meaningful (for criteria such as fundamental dominance, fundamental efficiency, adequacy, fundamental majorities, extremal majorities, ranking principles, and the comparison of inequalities in ordinal utilities).[13]

On the other hand, the position of this book was to discard, as meaningless, the concept of a cardinal utility that would be intrinsic, general, and for all purposes, or that could have the hedonistic meaning necessary for most direct social ethical applications. Yet, there can be such a hedonistic cardinal utility for the cases of weak preferences—see below—, as well as cardinal specifications of utility for particular purposes, such as "rational" choice in uncertainty—the von Neumann-Morgenstern theory—or, possi-

---

13. Adequacy is basically the conception of distributive justice that was favored in Antiquity: Give a thing to the person who can make the best out of it. Other concepts are based on the fact that fundamental preferences and utility permit permutations of individuals.

bly, other "independence" structures of social evaluation functions (additive separabilities). This implies discarding as meaningless a number of normative principles or criteria such as utilitarianism in its classical universal and hedonistic understanding, Nash's "bargaining solution" (as derived by Nash), or the Raiffa-Kalai-Smorodinski-Gauthier solution.[14]

Therefore, the general position is the use of interpersonally comparable preferences and utility, and the prima facie rejection of cardinal utility, in both cases in the name of meaningfulness and with qualifications (the first two parts of this book use none of these assumptions). I have explained these issues several times,[15] but it may be relevant again to say something about them here. Finally, I will also recall here how rationality answers the basic question of the analysis of justice, *why equality,* which is a preliminary requirement of the question of determining

---

14. These three forms have also been derived from particular theories which use the noted cardinal specification meaningful for choices in uncertainty, and also use other structures for utilitarianism. The logical and normative validity has then to be appraised in each case (see *Modern Theories of Justice*, op. cit., chap. 12 and 14).

15. See "The Optimal Production of Social Justice," op. cit.; *Justice and Equity*; "The Impossibility of Utilitarianism," in *The Good and the Economical* (P. Koslovski and Y. Shionoya eds., Springer Verlag, Heidelberg, 1993): 30-66; "The Meaning of Fundamental Preferences," *Social Choice and Welfare* 11(3) (1994): 193-8; *Modern Theories of Justice*, op. cit.

what to equalize among whom (be it rights and freedoms or goods or welfare).[16]

2 Fundamental Preferences and Utility

2.1 Meanings of Preferences and Utility

It should first be recalled that utility functions, or the more general preference orderings which may be representable by such functions, have always been taken to mean several possible things. Let us first recall here that a pairwise relation constitutes a preordering when it has the properties of antisymmetry and symmetry ("*a* more than *b*," "*b* more than *a*," and "*a* as much as *b*," exclude each other, and "*a* as much as *b*" implies "*b* as much as *a*"), and transitivity ("*a* more than *b*" and "*b* more than *c*" implies "*a* more than *c*," and the extensions when either one of the first two relations or all three relations are replaced by "as much as"). It is essential to remark that the use of the terms "more," "less," and "as much as" in common language practically implies the relations of antisymmetry and symmetry, and strongly suggests the transitivities.

In one of the classical meanings of utility or preference, each value (level) of utility, or each subset of indifferent alternatives, represents a level of a *substantive* or *tangible*

---

16. See Kolm, *The General Theory of Justice* (CERAS, Paris, 1990); "Distributive Justice," in *A Companion to Political Philosophy* (R. Goodin and P. Pettit eds., Basil Blackwell, Oxford, 1993): 438-61; *Equal Liberty*, op. cit.

individual state of experience such as satisfaction, happiness, well-being, possibly pleasure, sometimes welfare, or, often more relevantly and with an inverse relation, suffering, pain, displeasure, or distress. These concepts are indeed amenable to comparisons by related relations of more, less, or as much as, with the above noted implications providing the properties of a preordering at least in certain domains and cases. Note that a widespread (and surprising) misconception considers that such a substantial meaning necessarily implies more structure than ordinalism –such as cardinalism or even a quantitative structure–: there is no reason for that (see section 3 below).

In a series of other meanings, preference orderings and utility functions are just structures of the set of *choices* or of the *"preferences"* of the individuals when they are "rational." "Rational" is given here this ad hoc, particular and original meaning ("rational" normally means "for a reason," and so the considered use of this term suggests that preferring a to b and b to c constitutes a good reason for preferring a to c).[17]

When the reference is exclusively to choice, this can be a purely behavioristic position, and the consistency of the observed choices with some ordering constitutes only a behavioral law which may be assumed (then there is no assumption that there exists a particular psychological entity called "preferences" that this behavior would be "reveal-

---

17. Deriving utility functions from preference orderings can be attributed to Wold. But these formal discussions bypassed completely what is important, that is, the psychological meanings of these entities.

ing"). However, more explicit psychology is often implied or considered, and this is necessary for a number of uses of the concepts, including both all the direct normative uses and a discussion to be recalled below where people are assumed to have "preferences" over items that they do not choose. The mere consideration of potential choices begins to open the "mental black box." Then the minimal psychology consists in merely explaining the symmetries, anti-symmetries and transitivities of the preference relation (constituting a preordering) by the avoidance of a kind of "cognitive dissonance" produced in the individual who violates them in actual or hypothetical choice or in the mere expression of preferences or in simply thinking about them (this dissonance consists, for example, in preferring a to b and b to a, or a to b, b to c and c to a, and the individual would feel ill at ease as a result of such a possibly "inconsistent" behavior or position).[18] But one can also assume more explicit *preferences* within the individual, which "direct" her choice when a choice is made, but which exist independently of the choice and certainly prior to it. This common position is one which will have to be considered below, because it underlies a certain proposition that considers that people have prefer-ences on items that they cannot choose, namely certain aspects of what they are. Remember, however, that philosophers as psychologically perceptive as Frege and

18. See Kolm, *Happiness-Freedom,*op. cit.; *The Philosophy of Econom-ics* (*La Philosophie de L'Economie*) (Presses Universitaires de France, Paris, 1986).

Wittgenstein were very surprised to see scholars assuming that choice and action "flow from preferences as water from a reservoir."[19]

The former, tangible meaning of utility or preferences relates to the latter conception of preference by way of the consideration that the individual prefers what makes her more satisfied or happier. This constitutes either a psychological hypothesis or a semantic adjustment between the concepts of preferences and of happiness or satisfaction. This meaning will be underlined by the expression "eudemonistic preferences." It can therefore also be related to choice, with the conclusion that the individual chooses what makes her more satisfied or happier. The latter may be a behavioral assumption, but it can also be a tautological

---

19. The theory of "revealed preferences," that is, of preferences "revealed by choice," is not clear about its own possible psychological meaning. Do preferences direct choice, even, possibly, unconsciously? Or are they just the form of choice? Or, perhaps, such discussions should be discarded in the name of the behaviorist principle, or because they would be sterile. The considerations of "maximizing behavior" are similarly ambiguous. They sometimes explicitly are metaphors meaning that the agent acts "as if" she were maximizing something, irrespective of the possible reasons for this behavior. One may even discard the consideration of such reasons in the name of behaviorism. But, then, this assumption begs justification (this justification might be the "cognitive dissonance" elimination of intransitivities discussed earlier). In other cases, however, the agent is seen as moved by a kind of urge to maximize something, or by the will to do so, a conception which goes in the direction of "tangible" preferences, but without an explicitly stated psychological content.

consequence of including this property in the definition of happiness or satisfaction.

It should be noted that the assumption that individuals' preferences constitute an ordering (a preordering), hence "individual rationality" in this particular sense, strictly understood, cannot be falsified by experiments about choices that would "reveal" these preferences.[20] Indeed such a falsification by opposite pairwise preferences, intransitivity, other cyclicity, or choices that imply them, requires at least two experiments that are not performed at exactly the same time, and one can say that the preferences are dated and that the dated preferences have changed. Falsification requires, in addition, a certain hypothesis of continuity or stability. Hence, standard preference orderings or utility functions, strictly understood, are "metaphysical" concepts in Popper's sense. Yet, they are definitely useful and worthy conceptual tools. But they could not be strictly opposed to "fundamental preferences" (see below) on the ground that the latter may not be "revealed by choices."

Finally, social ethics can make a direct or an indirect use of concepts of individual preferences or utility. In the direct uses, these concepts represent an end value of this ethic, notably happiness or lower suffering, or satisfaction, and possibly pleasure. The indirect uses can utilize any meanings of these concepts, in particular they can utilize utility and preferences as merely representing or explaining choices (that is, they can utilize them more or less

---

20. See *The Philosophy of Economics*, op. cit.

behavioralistically, but these choices may be only potential). For example, the latter meaning suffices when the
end value of equal liberty is described by no individual
preferring another's allocation or situation to her own: this
social ethical principle then is an eleutherism rather than a
eudemonism, in spite of its presentation with preferences or
utilities.

2.2 Comparison of Satisfaction or Happiness

The normative uses of interpersonal comparability in "The
Optimal Production of Social Justice" (1966, op. cit.) and
in *Justice and Equity* basically required a tangible meaning
that can be an objective end value of social ethics, such as
happiness, satisfaction, or, with reverse order, suffering or
distress. Let us use the notion of happiness as an example
and because it has classically been taken as the proper
individual ethical end concept (Aristotle says that only
eudaemonia cannot be a means to something else). The
possibility of ranking the happiness of different individuals
raises three alternative positions about the question whether
an individual is happier, less happy, or as happy as another:

1. One can always answer.

2. One can never answer.

3. One can sometimes answer.

Position 1 is obviously wrong. But does it remain
wrong with sufficient information?

Position 2 can rest on two possible reasons, which may in fact be the same. One possible reason is that one never has sufficient information. The other reason is that happiness is an intimate experience, unique to each individual and absolutely incomparable by nature between different individuals. This may indeed amount to insurmontable lack of the information that would permit the comparison.[21]

Position 3 seems obvious to me. Compare for example a deportee in the Auschwitz concentration camp in 1943 with, say, a Malibu beach surfer. To argue that one cannot rank their happiness or their suffering because this is an intimate experience or because we lack information seems insane. Especially when the objective of these concepts is to provide a moral guidance to policy, notably about who should be helped first. But position 3 will be sufficient for the meaningfulness and definition of fundamental preferences and utility. Hence the only alternative to admitting these concepts is the delicate, subtle and cautious position of "Auschwitz agnosticism."

Information clearly plays a role in the determination of the scope or domain of the possibility of such pairwise comparisons. One indeed cannot tell if one does not know anything about the two compared persons. You may also not be able to say which of two persons is happier, or if they are equally happy, while a common mother or a common friend may see a clear answer. (Information may

---

21. The French classical scholarly tradition called the hypothesis of intrinsic incomparability "*le* no-bridge," thus referring to some forgotten discussion by English-speaking scholars.

indeed have to make the criterion itself more precise: for
instance, one person may be more serene and the other
more excited).

As noted earlier, only limited and generally available
information about such comparisons is necessary for
helping the most distressed people when this is required,
notably in a large society. Other applications require more
extended comparisons.

Let us thus consider the happiness, say, of persons-in-
situation. A person-in-situation is a person in a certain
state of society or of the world (including what the various
persons have or are in, and even what the other persons
are). Different persons-in-situation can be different persons
in different situations. They can also be the same person
in different situations. Persons-in-situation may be actual
or counterfactual. Let us say that there is eudemonistic
ranking comparability in a pair of persons-in-situation if
one can say whether one of these two persons-in-situation
is happier or less happy than the other, or whether each is
as happy as the other. The three alternatives are mutually
exclusive as required by natural language. Call this relation
the eudemonistic rank comparison.   When these two
persons-in-situation are the same person in different
situations, this describes the relation of happiness of this
person (possibly representable by her eudemonistic preferences or utility). The natural language of "more," "less,"
and "as . . . as" also strongly suggests that this relation is
transitive (A is happier than B and B is happier than C
implies that A is happier than C, with obvious extentions to
include the cases of "as happy as"). At any rate, consider
a subset of the set of persons-in-situation where the eude-

monistic rank comparison constitutes a complete preordering (which amounts to the corresponding rankings and transitivities). If this subset contains several persons (rather than only the same person in different situations), then this preordering is, by definition, a fundamental preference ordering. If this preordering is representable by an ordinal function, this function is, by definition, a fundamental utility function.

The ranked items (and the arguments of the function) are pairs of a person and of a corresponding situation. Several of these persons-in-situation may be the same person in different situations. Then the fundamental preference ordering coincides with this person's eudemonistic preference ordering, and any specification of the fundamental utility function is a specification of this person's (eudemonistic) utility function. A transformation of a specification of the fundamental utility function into another specification by an arbitrary increasing function, amounts to a transformation of the corresponding specifications of the persons' utility functions into other specifications by the same arbitrary increasing function (which thus is the same for all). This constitutes co-ordinalism and its justification. For certain problems, it may be that the relevant "situation" of a person is restricted to her "consumption" in the classical sense of economics. Finally, an individual can be described by her relevant characteristics, which are her capacities that make or enable her to derive satisfaction or happiness from the situation. These capacities are physical or mental. They include those that induce perception and sensation, permit the individual to perform the relevant activity, or put her in the relevant state. They can be represented by their causes (such as education, training or past experience in addition to natural endowments), or summarized by concepts such as "tastes." They include "appreciative capacities," "satisfaction capacities," "eudemonistic and hedonistic capacities," and so on.

Hence the existence of a fundamental preference ordering is uncontroversial, as is that of a fundamental utility function when this ordering admits of such a representation. The only possible issue concerns their domain of definition. This depends essentially on the scope and domain of eudemonistic ranking comparability. We have seen that this domain depends primarily on the relevant information. One can of course consider the concepts with hypothetical information. The question of whether the domain could be complete with "full" information (possibly including precision of the criterion of happiness or satisfaction) is of little practical interest since actual applications will never need a complete domain.[22]

2.3 Causes of Satisfaction or Happiness

The foregoing definition of fundamental preferences and fundamental ordinal utility is based on *comparison*. Another approach, based on *causality*, leads to the same result and indeed amounts to the same thing, but it first focusses on the relation from the person and the situation

---

22. However, the epistemic possibility and meaning of assuming a wide comparability is analyzed in "The Meaning of Fundamental Preferences," op. cit.

to the level of "happiness" rather than on the comparison between levels. The happiness (or any of the alternative individual states or feelings) of a person-in-situation is caused and determined, as everything is. Its level as a function of its causes is the fundamental utility. The preordering structure defined by the relations "more," "less," "as . . . as" with the implied transitivities is a priori meaningful for the phenomenon of happiness, and if only this structure is considered (and, possibly, is meaningful) this function is ordinal. This function is a usual univalued utility function if this ordering can be so represented, and a lexicographic set of indices in the general case (which may be relevant). The causes divide in two categories: the person's situation, and her propensity and capacity to be happy in a given situation, for instance her capacities to enjoy or to be satisfied, which can be replaced by their own causes (education, past experiences, or natural characteristics). A number of psychological studies have analyzed how sentiments such as satisfaction or happiness depend on these two kinds of variables, notably on general or specific past experiences, education, culture, and the type of character, in considering the outcome on an ordinal scale: these studies produce the (ordinal) fundamental utility function. Of course, the specification of the considered sentiment or state (of happiness or satisfaction, etc.) may matter more or less. Note that psychology is concerned with the human being, not with specific individuals as such.

The main point in the causal definition of fundamental preferences or utility is that the item whose causes are considered is happiness or satisfaction and not individuals' preference orderings, ordinal utility functions, or tastes revealed by choices or by preference rankings. The latter items are of course also caused, and their causes can be considered, but the consideration of their causation alone would not provide the interpersonal rank comparisons of individual levels of happiness or satisfaction, which are characteristic of the fundamental preferences and utility. If we only obtained that individuals have the same preference ordering over a suitably extended set of variables, this would not imply that a given indifference set corresponds to the same level of satisfaction or happiness for the various individuals; and if this ordering has a representation by an ordinal utility function, there would a priori be no meaning in using the same specification of this function for the various individuals (while the same specification results from the very eudemonistic interpersonal comparisons that define the fundamental utility). In particular, the causal definition of fundamental preferences or utilities has to consider *tangible* resulting states or sentiments (happiness, satisfaction, etc.) and not only the pure, naked and abstract preference orderings (which, at any rate, could not be "revealed by choice" as the classical behaviorist advocacy of such a concept has it, since individuals do not choose to be themselves or somebody else—although they can choose a number of their traits).

The fundamental preferences and utility present in the third part of *Justice and Equity* are justified both by eudemonistic rank comparison and by causality, as shown notably by the frequent reference—as the meaning of preference or utility—to tangible happiness with ordinal ranking (preorder).

2.4 Comparative Substitution

A few scholars have tried to justify a result formally identical to fundamental utility by a very different concept called "extended sympathy." Their motivation was to keep to the formal, abstract meaning of preferences, although the standard reason for this concept, the notion of preferences "revealed by choices," is irrelevant for interpersonal comparison because individuals do not choose to be themselves or somebody else. Consider individuals-in-situation denoted as A, B, C, D, etc. (the discussion is about the issue presently considered, rather than about individual preferences only, only if these individuals are not all the same individual in different situations). Individuals do sometimes express, and can sometimes feel, preferences for being or for not being someone else, or for being a certain person rather than another one. They might thus order (or preorder) individuals-in-situation. But these preferences seem prima facie to depend on who feels or expresses them. Individual A may prefer to be C rather than D, and B may prefer to be D rather than C. However, "A prefers to be B rather than C" actually means: "A prefers to be B rather than C, given that she is A." But "to be B given that one is A" can be seen as entailing a kind of contradiction. In particular, if individual A prefers to be B rather than C, and individual B prefers to be C rather than to be B (herself), if individual A became B rather than C, in agreement with her preferences, she would now prefer to be C rather than to be B. Or, individual A may prefer to be B rather than A (herself), while individual B prefers to be A rather than B (herself). In such cases, one individual wishes something which implies that she wishes the converse. Consistency is certainly at stake (with the possible cognitive dissonance caused by its violation, noted above). Similar considerations can involve transitivity (such as: A prefers to be B who prefers to be C who prefers to be A) or longer cycles, although the corresponding consistency issue is weaker.[23] Now, what fundamental preference wants is the preferability comparison between "to be B if one is B" (a possibly tautological expression) and "to be C if one is C" (idem). If there is some objective ranking of happiness of persons-in-situation, eudemonistic preferences constitute the fundamental preferences, and one is led to the considerations of section 2.

Such preferences about what one is, rather than only about what one has, are indeed common, including preferences about one's preferences and their causes. Yet at some point they raise the issue of information in a particularly acute manner. People commonly have preferences about aspects of what they are, and not only about what they have and the other aspects of the "situation." They wish they were taller, stronger, more beautiful or intelligent, had a better memory, and so on. They also have preferences about their preferences: they wish they preferred more easily available items; they regret their expensive tastes; they regret they cannot appreciate one thing or the other; they may even regret their own bad taste; and

---

23. A solution can be found in a psychological elimination of a cognitive dissonance elicited by the noted inconsistencies (with sufficient information).

they may regret their regret; they commonly regret or appreciate the education, experience, or habits that shaped their preferences, or wish they had been one way or the other. They feel and express such preferences, and they act in consequence by training or trying. Various such aspects of what they are even have a money value for people in the form of their willingness to pay. People also sometimes wish they were someone else, or are satisfied not to be this other person, or would prefer to be some person A rather than some other person B. However, actually fundamental preferences for interpersonal comparison more specifically require comparisons of "how it feels" to be A and of "how it feels" to be B. We have noted that ranking by preference based on such comparisons are sometimes unambiguous, and that this suffices for the most important problems. The existence of the sentiment of *compassion* proves that such eudemonistic interpersonal ranking is possible (at least for recognizing that certain people are less "happy" than one is). *Empathy* is, more generally, an existing phenomenon, but what would be required here is the further step of *comparative empathy*. One of the most elaborate parts of modern philosophy is *hermeneutics*, that is, trying to see and understand the world as certain other persons do (see, for instance, the works of Dilthey, Gadamer, or Ricoeur). This certainly implies feeling or appreciating the world as other persons do (although this evaluative attitude is not generally emphasized), and, again, what would be required here is comparison, which is usually not considered by these studies. The development of a comparative evaluation hermeneutics could make a notable contribution to the bases of social ethics.

2.5 History

In brief, fundamental preferences and fundamental utility can be justified by tangible eudemonistic *comparison* and *causality*. "Extended sympathy" tries to justify a concept that is formally the same by *comparative substitution*; this can be valid only with further considerations, hypotheses and discussion presented in the previous section, and in the end by bringing this view to the previous justification of fundamental preference and utility.

Work with fundamental preferences and utility is "fundamental analysis." It is commonly practiced in theoretical, empirical and applied economics, with both positive and normative uses, and in informal comparisons. Most authors who use this concept, however, seem not to care for meaning and justification. Indeed, most authors seem to think that fundamental preferences and utility can result from indexing the preference ordering or the utility function by the individual, whereas it can only result from a rank comparison of different individuals' indifference subsets or utility levels. Explicit attempts at justification are almost all concentrated on the normative applications (with only one exception which, however, does not explicitly compare levels of satisfaction). Fundamental preferences are presented and analyzed in my works of 1966, 1971, 1991, 1994, 1996.[24] They constitute a priori an ordering, possibly representable by an ordinal (fundamental) utility

---

24. Op. cit. and *Fundamental Analysis* (CERAS, Paris, 1991).

function. Other concepts considered indifference, cardinal utility, or "extended sympathy."

Tinbergen (1957) discusses fundamental indifference loci for tangible eudemonistic comparisons (he suggests asking specialists of this field, such as nurses, about comparisons of suffering or relief). Harsanyi (1953 and following works) considers a *cardinal* fundamental utility, which he uses as the von Neumann-Morgenstern utility for choices in uncertainty by the maximization of the mathematical expectation. The association of an ordinal fundamental utility and of a cardinal specification indeed provides and justifies a fundamental cardinal utility, when this cardinal specification is itself justified (which is the case for this particular cardinal utility for "rational" choices in uncertainty).[25] Harsanyi's work of 1953 considers what Rawls later called an "original position," and the fundamental utility is indeed the utility of an individual in the original position, "behind the veil of ignorance," who does not know which actual individual she will be and thus has preferences about actual individuals-in-situation and thus in particular about the various possible actual selves; what is questionable here is the validity of original position theories.[26] Harsanyi later emphasized, as justification, causality and, implicitly, hermeneutics (Taylor). Becker and Stigler (1977) is the only work noted here that does not

---

25. See Kolm, *The Impossibility of Utilitarianism* (CGPC, Paris, 1992).

26. See Kolm, *Modern Theories of Justice*, op. cit., chap. 8; and "Rational Just Social Choice," in *Social Choice Revisited* (K. Arrow et al. eds., Macmillan, London, 1996, vol. 2): 167-95.

consider normative applications. Their justification is
causality, but, as with Harsanyi's use of this justification,
they do not point out that causality justifies fundamentalism
only if applied to a tangible outcome (such as satisfaction
and happiness) while it does not if it applies to preference
orderings or to classical utility functions. Arrow (1977,
following a suggestion of 1963) takes the position of
"extended sympathy" (which he named). Suppes (1957,
1966) more or less uses, rather than justifies, the fundamental concept. Extended sympathy has been criticized by
Broome (a largely valid criticism mistakenly aimed at
fundamental utility) and by Hausman.[27]

3 Cardinal Utility

The concept whose use was rejected in *Justice and Equity*
is that of a cardinal utility, for the following reason which
shows its lack of general meaningfulness (although certain
cardinal specifications of a utility function have meaning
for particular issues or situations). A fortiori, quantitative

---

27. See J. Tinbergen, "Welfare Economics and Income Distribution,"
American Economic Review 47 (1957): 490-503; J. Harsanyi, "Cardinal
Utility in Welfare Economics and in the Theory of Risk-Taking,"
Journal of Political Economy 61 (1953): 434-35; G. Becker and G.
Stigler, "De Gustibus Non Est Disputandum," *American Economic
Review* (1977); K. Arrow, "Extended Sympathy and the Possibility of
Social Choice," *American Economic Review* 67 (1977): 219-25; P.
Suppes, "Some Formal Models of Grading Principles," *Synthese* 16
(1966): 284-306.

utility (utility having the logical properties of a quantity) was rejected.

A utility function $u(a)$ for a given individual is considered. By definition, it is cardinal if it is defined only up to an increasing linear (affine) transformation. With the required topological assumptions about the connexity of the range of definition (which need not retain us here as in most applications), cardinality of $u(a)$ is equivalent to the invariance of each of the three following properties with respect to the specification of the function u, for any given items a, b, c, d and constant k:

$$u(a) - u(b) > u(c) - u(d) \tag{1}$$

$$u(a) - u(b) = k \cdot [u(c) - u(d)] \tag{2}$$

$$u(a) - u(b) > k \cdot [u(c) - u(d)] \tag{3}$$

where the k are constants depending only on a, b, c, d, and the sign $>$ can be replaced by $\geq$.[28] The issue thus is the actual meaning of these formulas. "Actual" means here referring to psychology (or behavior) and not only to mathematics.

Formula 1 is usually taken to mean "I prefer a to b more than I prefer c to d." Such an expression is indeed sometimes actually meaningful (for example and at least, it is when I am almost indifferent between c and d and not

---

28. See "The Impossibility of Utilitarianism," op. cit., and the literature quoted there.

between a and b). But, then, and this is the crucial point, there is no reason or justification to write this comparison as the comparison of *differences* in utility levels. There is no reason to translate "I prefer a to b" by $u(a) - u(b)$.

The sometimes meaningful comparison is only a comparison of pairwise preference comparisons. The following considerations are necessary if cardinal utility were to be made sense of in this manner. The comparisons of pairwise preferences may constitute a preordering. This preordering may be representable by an ordinal function U, such that "I prefer a to b more than I prefer c to d" is $U(a, b) > U(c, d)$, with $u(a) > u(b)$ and $u(c) > u(d)$. A discussion shows that a case worthy of consideration is that where the items enter the function U only by their utility level, that is, U can be written as $U(a, b) = V[u(a), u(b)]$ with a function V which is increasing in $u(a)$ and decreasing in $u(b)$. But this is as far as one can go in general in the direction of the justification of cardinal utility, and this falls short of this justification. If there were an increasing function f such that, with $v = f(u)$, one would have $U = V = W[v(a) - v(b)]$, one could replace the ordinal U by the difference $v(a) - v(b)$. But the function v is a specification of the function u (which is a priori ordinal). Then, the function v would be a cardinal utility which would be actually meaningful and actually justified by the comparison of pairwise preferences. But in general there is no such function f leading to a function W.

Furthermore, relation 2 would have to be justified by expressions of the type "I prefer a to b 2.8 times more than I prefer c to d", which a priori does not seem to be actually meaningful.

There are other properties of preferences which make them more specific than mere ordinal concepts, but these properties do not lead to cardinality (for example, the second degree "{I prefer a to b more than c to d} more than {I prefer e to f more than g to h}" is sometimes meaningful—for instance when there is almost indifference within the pairs c and d, e and g, and f and h, but not between a and b.

However, for certain cases and issues, certain concepts of cardinal preferences have meaning. The most important is that cardinal utility can be justified as indicated above for *weak preferences*, that is, for preferences that tend to indifference. Then, one can show that the function f defined as $f(x) = \int^x V_1(y,y)\, dy$, where V_1 is the first derivative of the function $V(x,y)$ previously considered, defines a justified cardinal utility $v = f(u)$.[29]

Cardinal forms are also met when the variables contain comparable subsets of variables (such as with different eventualities or different dates), with a property of independence (preferences concerning one subset do not depend on the given other subsets) which implies an additive separability of a specification of the ordinal utility function. Then, the added functions are cardinal (with at least the same arbitrary multiplicative factor). Relatedly, the theory of "rational" choice in uncertainty by the maximization of the expected utility (von Neumann-Morgenstern) uses a meaningfully cardinal utility in certainty to build up the full

---

29. See *Modern Theories of Justice*, op. cit., chap. 12.

utility in uncertainty, but this meaningfulness is restricted
to this use.

The general meaninglessness of cardinal utility rules out
a number of well-known definitions of the optimum
(including utilitarianism, although there are a number of
"utilitaromorphisms" which should each be evaluated
separately).[30]

**4   Summary of Issues in Comparison of Utilities or
Preferences**

The main issues about the comparison of preferences and
utilities are now summarized.

Two entities have to be distinguished:

-   The levels of "utility," satisfaction, happiness, suffering,
    distress, etc., which constitute a priori an ordinal
    concept (ordering of levels).
-   The preferences.

    The preferences can correspond to the levels.
    There are two general issues:

-   The comparisons, which can be intrapersonal or inter-
    personal.
-   Causes.

---

30.   See *Modern Theories of Justice*, op. cit., chap. 14.

The issues are the following, all concerning a priori ordinal items:

1. Intrapersonal comparison of levels, which may constitute the individual preferences.
2. Interpersonal comparison of levels, which lead to fundamental preferences.
3. Interpersonal comparison of orderings or of ordinal utility functions.
4. Causes of levels (including satisfaction capacities), which leads to fundamental preferences.
5. Original position, which provides fundamental preferences, but constitutes a rather extraordinary concept.
6. Preferences about one's self.
7. Conceptual substitution of selves, leading to empathy.
8. Comparative empathy, which is possible in certain cases as shown by the sentiment of compassion.
9. Preferences among various actual selves, which do not imply per se fundamental preferences, but raise problems of consistency that are waived by fundamental preferences, and lead to fundamental preferences when the comparison bears on eudemonistic levels.
10. Intrapersonal comparison of pairwise preferences, which does not justify cardinal utility except for weak preferences.
11. Interpersonal comparison of pairwise preferences, which yields a utilitarian form for weak preferences and exists only in certain cases of local justice (microjustice).[31]

---

31. See *Modern Theories of Justice*, op. cit., chap. 14.

12. Comparison of comparisons of pairwise preference comparisons in cases 10 and 11, and possibly higher orders of comparisons.

5 Why Equality? Equality as Rationality

The last issue that needs to be made precise here concerns the status of equality. Equality can be of many things, such as goods or welfare, or rights, freedoms or powers of many kinds (modern social ethics is based on the principle that men are "free and equal in rights"). But the issue "Equality of what?" is second to the more basic one: "Why equality?"

If I give a piece of bread to someone because she lacks three hundred calories, with no further reason or qualification, and I refuse to give a similar piece of bread (which I have) to someone else who also lacks three hundred calories, my behavior will be deemed unjust, arbitrary and irrational. I take it that it is unjust because it is irrational in the field of justice, and justice has to be justified. Note that the term "rational" is used here in its standard sense of "for a reason."

More generally if, for a certain issue, what is attributed to someone depends only on certain characteristics of hers and not on others' allocations and characteristics, two persons who have the same relevant characteristics should receive the same thing, as a consequence of rationality in the normal sense of "for a reason." The reason is indeed based on the relevant characteristics, and it yields the same conclusion for two persons with identical relevant characteristics.

If now I have one piece of bread and I divide it in proportions (1/3, 2/3) between two persons whose characteristics deemed to be relevant for this issue are identical, then I cannot relevantly distinguish this sharing from the converse one (2/3, 1/3), and hence I can provide no reason for choosing one rather than the other. Only equal sharing such as (1/2, 1/2) avoids this particular lack of a reason, or irrationality (or arbitrariness). This holds whatever the basis, and indeed the presence or absence, of other reasons for this allocation.

Hence this indistinguishability of permutation provides the basis for facing two questions, although it may be that only one of them is relevant in a given context. First, what a person should receive may be seen as depending not only on her relevant characteristics, but also on others' allocations and characteristics, for instance as a consequence of comparisons. Second, there may not be a tangible reason for the choice of allocation, and we will see that even in this case there is a reason for equality.

The problem is to make the rational choice of allocation (of any nature) to persons (or, more generally, "justiciable" social entities) in any number. Rational means justified by reason, or non-arbitrary—the normal meaning of the term. The choice is meant for implementation, that is, to guide action (hence the field is practical reason in Kant's sense). This choice is among alternatives defined as mutually exclusive, that is, only one can exist. Therefore, the choice has to select a unique state.

We now and henceforth consider persons with identical relevant characteristics. These characteristics include all that could relevantly differentiate one person from the other (apart from their considered allocation). They include in particular all that is deemed necessary and relevant to base the moral judgment, but they can also include other elements such as considerations of possibility.

Several states which differ only by permutations of these persons' allocations are called permuted states. Permuted states cannot be distinguished from one another, a result of the definition of the identical characteristics. Hence one cannot justify choosing one state rather than any of its permuted states. Also, if the choice of one state is justified, so is the choice of any of its permuted states. But permuted states are actually different states if at least one same person receives different allocations in them. Therefore, the choice of a state can be justified and unique only if each person receives the same allocation in all its permuted states, that is to say if all persons have identical allocations. This is equality. Hence this equal treatment of equals is a necessary consequence of practical reason (i.e., of the requirement to fully justify the unique choice necessary for action). There may be several possible states with equality, and then the choice among them requires further considerations, but the point here is that the choice should be with equality (in many problems, one such state defined with the relevant variables dominates all others).

This result answers the two questions posed. First, sufficiently justified choice implies equal treatment of equals even if the reasons provided for each individual's allocation refer not only to this individual's characteristics but also to others' characteristics or allocations. Second, if there are no other reasons for the allocations, or if such reasons are not yet or not explicitly provided, then the above reasoning provides a reason for equality.

Before further discussion of this latter point, we may have to note that the use of a lottery cannot constitute a solution. Lotteries can be used either for choosing among permuted states, or for choosing one state among all possible ones in the absence of a sufficient reason. But first, one would have to choose the *ex ante* distribution of probabilities, and this is precisely an instance of the problem whose solution is being sought. The standard proposal would be to choose equal probabilities. But even when this is well defined (as for the permutations with a finite number of persons), this equality has to be justified. If it is, such a justification can directly be applied to the allocation problem initially considered. In fact, the justification of equality in the absence of another, tangible reason, to be discussed shortly, relies precisely on not using a lottery to face the issue of the indistinguishability of permuted states. It would thus be inconsistent to use both such a lottery and this justification for the equality of probabilities. Equivalently, the use of lotteries to chose probabilities entails an infinite regress. Second, a lottery does not constitute a reason. One could even add that it relies on phenomena irrelevant to the issue considered (such as the dynamics of falling bodies in the flipping of a coin)–although this remark raises the issue of the notion of "pure chance." Lottery can only be a second-best allocative method, for instance in the case of indivisibilities. It then basically rests on the justification of equality to be discussed shortly, for the choice of *ex ante* probabilities, and indeed for the very basic "axiom" of the definition of a probability (the Laplace, or Condorcet or Bayes, principle of "nonsufficient reason" of choosing equal probabilities in complete ignorance).[32]

Let us thus now come back to the case where "there is no other reason." That is, there is no reason given a priori, external to the *sui generis* structural logic of the situation, that could lead to the choice of one of the possible states rather than of any other. Then, two remarks can be presented, both of which make states with equality different from others.

First, we know that if there were a reason for making the choice, it would designate a state with equality, for the reasons presented above (let us remember that we consider persons with identical relevant characteristics). This holds whatever the nature of this reason. One may then consider that there has to be a reason of some kind, because a choice has to be made (among the mutually exclusive alternatives, one of which will be the actual state of the world), but we a priori know that the outcome of this reason has to be equality, and this information suffices. One may more specifically consider that the absence of a reason actually means the ignorance of the reason, and the reason, whatever it is, would lead to equality–this is the only thing we know about it, and we indeed need not know more.

---

32. Hence the vindication of equality presented here constitutes also a contribution to the foundations of probability, whereby the Laplace principle is not a primitive axiom but a consequence of rationality and of the uniqueness of the probability measure.

Moreover, the impossibility of providing a reason for choosing one state rather than any of its permuted states constitutes a precise, well defined, and specific lack of rationality, or irrationality, that ceases to exist only for states with equality (that are identical to their permuted states). Any absence of equality entails this irremediable irrationality or arbitrariness, irrespective of all the rest of our knowledge. And there is no other reason or lack of reason that would favor any choice other than equality, either, by assumption, in the field of external, a priori or tangible reasons, or in the field of purely logical, intrinsic and structural reasons such as the difference just considered. Hence, one may consider that a principle of minimal irrationality, or minimal arbitrariness, leads one to choose equality. All choices are arbitrary by assumption, but equality is less arbitrary than others in the noted sense. Equality, indeed, stands alone in having one less reason for arbitrariness than other alternatives. Thus, even in the absence of any tangible reason, this minimal irrationality can provide a reason for preferring equality. The nature of this reason is rationality itself: The mere requirement of providing a reason provides by itself the reason.

This doubtlessly constitutes the reason why, in the absence of other reasons, equality is actually chosen and preferred, and is deemed less arbitrary and more just than inequality (justice has to be justified). Even though this reason is intuitively felt rather than fully articulated. Indeed, popular arguments commonly refer to permutation to prove arbitrariness and lack of reason ("why give this to him rather than to her?").

The foregoing reasoning is very different from the classical position "if there is no reason for inequality, choose equality." This view can be read in Aristotle (*Nichomachean Ethics*), Hobbes (*Leviathan*), Locke (*Second Treatise on Government*, with the expression "If God wanted us to choose inequality, he would have given us a sign"), Condorcet (project of a Declaration of Rights, 1789), Sidgwick, and in modern times Isaiah Berlin and from him a number of scholars. A priori, it is not clear whether this expression is in the field of logic, and then possibly a tautology, or if it constitutes a moral position. But this cannot be a purely logical expression. Indeed, if it is stated, this implies that there is no other reason for equality that would be sufficient. Hence, that there are sufficient reasons neither for inequality nor for equality. Then, the same sentence can be applied in singling out any unequal state rather than equality, and it would enjoin choosing it: this "argument" "justifies" any inequality as well as equality. Therefore, this classical principle constitutes a purely moral position. Then, it may be accused of being arbitrary, unjustified. This is to be contrasted with the arguments of the preceding paragraphs, which are essentially logical ones. These arguments constituted an instance of the general philosophy that ethics should be fully justified and hence should be based solely on knowledge from outside ethics, notably rationality and logic, and possibly other fields.

Hence, equal treatment of equals in the relevant characteristics constitutes, or can be seen as, a requirement of rationality, which binds moral choices of justice as arithmetic does when I have to give you back due change. But the

relevant equality may be impossible, or it may interfere
with other criteria of social optimality, in particular with
the equality of other items that are also deemed relevant.
Hence, an equality is a priori only ideal, or prima facie,
that is, in the absence of an overpowering reason. Therefore, the general choice of justice consists in selecting the
various relevant principles, notably the various relevant
equalizands (that which should be equalized), and in
defining modes of adjustments when these ideals are not all
copossible. These adjustments can be of several logical
types, such as priorities, compromises, superimposition (that
is, application of a principle from the outcome of another,
such as equally free exchange from equal sharing), and so
on.[33] This leads one to various "second best egalitarian"
solutions. Among the principles having priority are the
guarantee of basic rights, the satisfaction of basic needs,
and Pareto-efficiency which is a type of equality of power
(and may have to be applied to preferences cleansed of
unethical features).[34]

The present work contains a number of applications of
these general principles, such as equal freedom, equally free
exchange from equal division, or leximin in fundamental
preferences or utility as the efficient second-best welfare or
eudemonistic egalitarianism.

---

33. The types of adjustments are analyzed in *The General Theory of
Justice*, op. cit.

34. The article "The Economics of Social Sentiments: The Case of
Envy," op. cit., shows how this cleansing can be precisely done in the
cases of envy, jealousy or other comparative sentiments.

Justice and Equity

Introduction

1 Toward a Formal Ethic

Ideas of justice, fairness, or equity of the type considered here have lingered in the minds of men for centuries, indeed for much longer. Undoubtedly one would find traces of them in the works of many thinkers like Aristotle, Aquinas, Hume, or Rousseau. Particularly, they would be found underlying the written and unwritten rules of justice of all ages and all people. The Salic law, the Code of Hammurabi, and the Bible would be obvious points of departure for this research through the law, cases, and ethnological reports. Moreover, these ideas would be discovered in the social behavior of people motivated by sentiments and sense of justice: a mother sharing or settling disputes among her children, the "rapports de bon voisinage" (good relations among neighbors), motivations and norms of "reciprocity," the customs or rules governing relations among members of diverse groups, and the motivations behind gifts, politeness, charity, and political involvement. They would be revealed in social sentiments or feelings like pity, empathy, and indignation against injustice. In fact, certain notions that we will treat probably have been felt since the dawn of human existence.

But this study utilizes scientific thought: it is therefore characterized by precise expression and by the abundance of relatively elaborate deductions. The first concrete step for achieving this objective is the use of a formal language. This is done largely thanks to the use and application of classical conceptual tools of economic analysis. That is one of the two ties between this study and economics. The second is that economic problems of distribution of commodities, income, and wealth cannot be resolved without considerations of justice and of equity.

2 Economic Justice

"It is only in the backward countries of the world that increased production is still an important objective; in the most advanced, what is needed from an economic perspective is a better distribution. . . ." This contesting of productionism is authorized by John Stuart Mill.[1] It dates from 1847.

Since then, production has grown tremendously, and yet almost no one, even in wealthier countries, dares to say that growth is no longer an important objective and that only distribution counts. But the output is distributed and its distribution matters, and if this distribution does not have promotion of production as sole objective, one of the reasons for this is that it seeks to satisfy other criteria which may be classified under the general name *social justice*. Few things, however, are a priori less well defined than these criteria, although few things are more important (people who claim to reject the very idea of social justice are in reality proposing one of their own which they just want us to think is "natural," whereas it certainly is as much a social artifact as any other). Is social justice equality? Why? Equality of what? Among whom? What is equality among people whose needs, conditions, and labors differ? Is it "to each according to her needs"? Once

---

1. *Principles of Political Economy*, book 4, chap. 6, sec. 2.

assured of the elementary necessities of survival and of life, what is a need? Does one wish, for example, to satisfy the "needs" of competing conspicuous consumption, which are by nature insatiable? Or is equality "to each according to her work," either because of a natural right in the product of one's capacities or in order to compensate for the discomfort of labor? Or else is it equality of liberties, prerogatives, and powers as intended by the founding republican principle "Men are free and equal in rights?"

Economists, who asked the question of the just distribution, have remarkably failed to answer it. Certainly, they have developed an impressive body of thought, Welfare Economics, the goal of which is to identify what *ought to* be done. Unfortunately, although they have a great deal to say about *efficiency* ("Pareto optimality"), they are nearly silent concerning meaningful principles of *justice*.[2] This deficiency is at once the great scandal of the discipline and a major obstacle to its social utility. In fact, all practical choices in society (for government actions, for example) involve sacrificing the well-being and the means of some for the benefit of others, as compared with alternatives that could have been chosen. Even if it is not the only thing that matters, the problem of justice is essential, omnipresent and inevitable.

Economists not only have failed to provide a solution, but, worse, they have tried harder to avoid the problem than

---

2. *Author's note of 1997*: Of course, much has been done since this sentence and the following text were published in 1971 (*Modern Theories of Justice*, op. cit., provides a critical survey).

to solve it. They have both focused on individual satisfactions and squandered treasures of ingenuity in the attempt
to rid themselves of the unhappy obligation of making
interindividual comparisons: efficiency criterion (unanimity, or "Pareto"); "*no bridge*" precluding interpersonal
comparisons of happiness, satisfaction, or utility; redistributive transfers supposedly "otherwise carried out"; "lump
sum taxes"; "principles of compensation"; a priori hypothesis of optimality of distribution; collective or social or state
utility functions; or hypothetically leaving the choice to
"the government." But all these efforts are in vain: the
efficiency criterion is insufficient; the redistributive transfers that should accompany various actions in fact are not
carried out and are sometimes not even logically capable of
being carried out;[3] the lump sum tax is either arbitrary or
impossible when ethics or information demands that the
policy be related to some relevant objective characteristics
of individuals which they can more or less affect; nothing
suggests that the distribution is optimal; there may be no
acceptable collective utility function;[4] the state or government utility function is not given to the economist and,
usually, does not even exist; and the normative acceptability

---

3. See Kolm, *L'Etat et le Système des Prix* (Editions Dunod, Paris,
1969), part 1.

4. See Arrow, *Social Choice and Individual Values* (Wiley, 1951, 1963).
However, the actual problem is to determine the social optimum in the
actual set of possible states and with the actual individual preferences (if
they are relevant), and not to determine a social ordering for any
individual preferences.

of a political authority's judgment depends on that of the political process that chooses the authority; finally, other procedures do not even pass the test of logical consistency (cf. the classical critiques of the "principle of compensation").[5]

Having failed to shun the problem of justice, economic science would do better to approach the problem head on and to look for ways of solution. Contrary to what many economists think, such ways do exist, and the opposite assertion would be lack of imagination (and even, in certain cases, a defense of an ideological interest in avoiding the discussion of the issue of justice). Indeed, the solutions presented here prove at least that a priori abdication is unjustified. Moreover, these principles constitute both the relevant criteria for many specific issues of justice and the core and basis of the general solution of the just structure of the allocation of rights and resources.

In "The Optimal Production of Social Justice,"[6] a number of solutions are proposed and two families of them are thoroughly worked out. Two other families of solutions are presented and analyzed here. Taken together, these texts provide the essentials of the topic, and the basis for further applications and perfectings. In particular, they provide the basic concepts and properties of the three great

---

5. Since the 1930s, by Hicks, Kaldor, Scitovsky, and many others.

6. 1966, International Economic Association Conference on Public Economics, Biarritz, proceedings edited by H. Guitton and J. Margolis, *Economie Publique* (CNRS, Paris, 1968), and *Public Economics* (Macmillan, London, 1969).

issues of distributive justice: equalities and inequalities in income, wealth or goods, in liberty or opportunity, and in happiness or satisfaction.

3 Objectives and Limits of This Study

But it may be useful to ward off some possible misunderstandings. To begin with, we will consider vocabulary. The title *Justice and Equity* corresponds precisely to the subject. This does not mean that one will find here an exhaustive presentation of all that has ever been thought, experienced or done that these terms would cover. That would, of course, be impossible. However, we just noted that this text and "The Optimal Production of Social Justice" provide the essentials of the main issues of distributive justice. Moreover, this text specializes in a particular perspective, but one which is nevertheless general. Its ambition is, in fact, that these two works present all that can be said to date on the subject that has justification, depth, generality, and precision.

To what extent does it succeed? Its going far beyond what has been written on the subject is hardly a measure of performance since there was so little that was actually acceptable (for instance, it will be shown that the moral uses of cardinal utility cannot be retained). On the other hand, this study does not say all that can be said, and there still are concepts and properties to be found in this field. This acknowledgment comes in part from the fact that the analyses presented do not suffice to completely resolve in detail the final problem posed, that is, to define with sufficient certainty all the specifics of all the aspects of the social optimum, while the problem necessarily has a solution since the solution should dictate the *choices of actions* that cannot be avoided. This view also comes from the experience of research: the fundamental conceptual ideas take years to develop; at any given moment, one is tempted to believe that one is at "the end of the rope," that one has said all that can be said; but one believed the same thing one or two ideas earlier, and, after some progress, extrapolation suggests that eventually one will go even further. It is still to be conjectured how far this analysis is from the goal in this text. The answer depends on the consideration of the importance of the properties and principles, and for the most important ones an overview of the general issue of justice suggests that it should not be very far.

Another warning also may be necessary. We will have to introduce certain concepts and properties, and give them names. Primarily this is to accomplish the facility of exposition which all sciences attempt. But, in addition, since we are interested here in concepts and properties having a meaning, either ethical or in "social logic," their names will naturally be chosen from among the words that express it the best. One problem is knowing whether a name is too "heavy" or too "light," too broad or too narrow for the idea, and conversely. On the other hand, when a concept already has been used and named, we endeavor to show an intelligent respect for this heritage.

We prefer the simple "efficient" and "efficiency" to complicated variations on Pareto's name (or even to the exact but weighty terms "maximal or maximality for unanimity"). When the words used to mention a concept have included "equity" and "equitable," we have kept these terms. In this case, however, the word is a priori somewhat broader than the idea. Certainly it is often used in other senses, although generally imprecisely, in contrast to the definition that we use. In other words, this definition *specifies* the concept. Nevertheless, this precise definition does not lack generality, and certainly people have often used the terms "equity" and "equitable" in the sense we will use them, although without taking the trouble entirely to explain their idea. Moreover, this concept is very basic, it amounts to and is related to deep kinds of equality, and "equity" just comes from the latin word for "equal."

The terms "just" and "justice" are broader still, but the precise concept to which we apply the name is general eudemonistic justice, or all-inclusive distributive justice in a sense (ideal equal sharing of the benefits from the bulk of all resources, including capacities to be satisfied), and hence it is itself extremely powerful. Enough, it seems, to support the term. That is why the properties that will use the basic idea of this concept of justice–a *deep* identity of human beings–will be attributed the adjective "fundamental." This term seems to be, contrary to the preceding ones, neutral from the point of view of "moral emotion." The same will be true of the names of several other concepts we will introduce, without this implying that their semantic content is poorer in ethical meaning: "adequacy," "dominance," etc.

This text is intended to be both complete and simple. To satisfy the first objective, it makes use—in addition to the new concepts it introduces—of a few notions that had already been noted (equity, "divide and choose," proposals having certain aspects of "fundamental preferences"). On the one hand, this is necessary in order to reach all of its original results. On the other hand, in general these ideas had been mentioned only briefly or in passing, each in separate texts, and without their properties, implications, consequences, applications, and relations among them and with other concepts receiving any attempt at investigation. Given their philosophic importance, it appeared necessary to analyze them exhaustively and in depth, and the rich harvest of properties which came out certainly justifies, *a posteriori*, the undertaking. And, of course, we have studied in much the same depth the new properties proposed.

This book even almost does the work of the reader on many points, in explicitly stating a large part of what she should have thought herself anyway in order to arrive at a complete understanding of the subject. The goal is thereby to minimize the work the reader must normally do in order to understand the properties and proofs, taking into account the constraint imposed by the necessity of setting forth the issue and employing a formalized language.

But this formalization is itself reduced to what is indispensable in order to present the social content of the subject, by avoiding all mathematical refinement which would be unjustified for lack of effective meaning for the ethical, social, human, and economic questions which interest us here. This allows us to stay on an altogether elementary mathematical level, a very important advantage since formalization, while it can greatly aid communication among those who comprehend it, also is a blocking obstacle to transmission of ideas among persons who are not equally accustomed to it. It is therefore a great opportunity to have been able to present these ideas, without losing anything of importance, with mathematics which, from the point of view of the mathematician, is "commonplace." But just because the mathematical form is elementary does not indicate that the actual content, which is by no means mathematical, also is, since it is almost always new, at the frontier of science, and is investigated in depth.

Finally, this text is accessible, more or less easily, to everyone who has some familiarity with formalization, and all the more if it is with the tools of economic analysis or of mathematical psychology. That is not yet everyone. But it has been attempted that it be the largest number of persons possible: everyone has a right to ideas.

4 History of Ideas and Review of the Literature on the Subject

We noted earlier the extent to which the intuition of certain of the ideas that will be studied probably is old and widespread. We also remarked that the passage to a precise formalization can constitute decisive progress. Formalization is in this case an infinitely more important jump than a simple "mise en forme." It is properly an innovation that belongs to scientific imagination. It is therefore interesting, for the history of thought, to note its stages.

The idea of what is called here *fundamental preferences* is necessarily used by anyone who dares compare individuals' welfares, happinesses, or satisfactions, and such comparisons are logically required and inescapable if these concepts are deemed to have any direct relevance to justice.

John Harsanyi used a concept akin to a cardinal fundamental utility in "Cardinal Utility in Welfare Economics and in the Theory of Risk-taking,"[7] while the fundamental preferences and utility functions used here and in "The Optimal Production of Social Justice"[8] are a priori purely ordinal notions (that is, their structure is only that of order, possibly with equivalences). Jan Tinbergen used a similar idea ordinally for equating levels of satisfaction in his brief address to the American Economic Association in December 1956.[9] It is symptomatic that the presentation of his excellent text to a public of American economists was, as theater people say, a "flop" (this was reported to me by Hendrik Houthakker, who presided over the meeting). This confirms the suspicion of cultural differences in interest about various concepts of justice, notably as concerns equality of results as opposed to equality of opportunities (Léon Walras wrote: "Justice is a Greco-Roman and French idea").

Fundamental preferences constitute one of the concepts presented in "The Optimal Production of Social Justice." It has been noted to me (by Professor Charles Fried of Harvard Law School) that the philosopher John Rawls is advocating views that may have a certain formal similitude with my concept of *practical justice* (the lexicographic maximin in fundamental preferences). But the similitude

---

7. *Journal of Political Economy* (1953).

8. Kolm, 1966, op. cit.

9. See "Papers and Proceedings," *American Economic Review* (May 1957).

seems to be closer with the maximin in income I also considered, as a nonuniversal criterion, in various works (including "The Optimal Production of Social Justice"). Rawls' essential point seems indeed to be very different from practical justice, since the end values of ideally egalitarian justice he considers are not individuals' final ends and appreciation of the world, and hence this distributive justice endorses the inequalities resulting from different capacities used in enjoyment and consumption while it takes the opposite first best position for capacities used in work and production.[10] Another difference is that practical justice is not meant to be applied universally, but only for appropriate problems of justice. Moreover, Rawls' universal end values of justice consist of several "goods" (one of which is income). But there seem to be logical difficulties in considering several such goods (rather than fundamental preferences), as well as in the reasons provided both for this scheme and for not reaching equality.

With regard to the concept of equity as no individual preferring any other's allocation to his own, Jan Tinbergen pointed out to me, at a conference in Paris in 1962 where I was presenting the theory of the comparison of inequalities, that it had been proposed several decades earlier by the Dutch physicist Ehrenfest (his professor) for defining the

---

10. *Author's note of 1997*: However, in 1982, Rawls discussed favorably *Justice et Equité* and in particular fundamental preferences and practical justice in "Social Unity and Primary Goods" (in *Utilitarianism and Beyond*, ed. by A. Sen and B. Williams, Oxford University Press, Oxford).

equitable wages for the various occupations.[11] This notion is probably noted for the first time in the economic literature in English by Duncan Foley as a cursory remark in his dissertation "Resource Allocation in the Public Sector"[12] for the distribution of commodities. A way of proof of the existence of one equitable and efficient distribution of given quantities of divisible and transferable goods has been noted by David Schmeidler (in collaboration with Menahem Yaari, it seems).

The ideas of unanimity and of majority are obvious. The concept of efficiency (Pareto optimality) is classical. Contrary to what has been asserted, it is properly attributed to Vilfredo Pareto. And he had much more to add on the subject.[13]

The process of "divide and choose," of which we analyze the properties, certainly has been long known and used. For example, it is said to be used in England for the division of inheritances. It is described in the classic book

---

11. Along with page proofs I receive the English translation of Jan Pen's book *Income Distribution*, just published. We learn here (p. 304) that the concept of "equity" is presented and discussed by Jan Tinbergen in his book in Dutch and not translated *Redelijke Inkomensverdeling* of 1953 [in fact the publication date was 1946].

12. *Yale Economic Essays*, no. 1, 1967.

13. *Author's note of 1997*: See Kolm, "The Optimal Production of Social Justice," op. cit.; *La Bonne Economie, La Réciprocité générale* (Presses Universitaires de France, Paris, 1984), chap. 11.

Games and Decisions, by Luce and Raiffa,[14] with an error
that will be mentioned later.

Finally, there are other propositions with analogous
purposes, and some propositions for extension to n persons
of the divide and choose process defined for two persons,
but they are not included or mentioned here because their
tangible content (social, economic, ethical, psychological,
and even logical) appears insufficient or non-existent.

Among the new concepts and results that will be met in
the present study, there are in particular the following:
fundamental dominance, fundamental equivalence, and
fundamental efficiency, their properties and their relations
with unanimity, efficiency, justice, equity, adequacy, and
ordinal inequality; practical justice, its properties and its
relations with unanimity, efficiency, justice, fundamental
dominance, fundamental efficiency, ordinal inequality, and
truncations; conditional and restricted practical justice;
adequacy and its relation with equity and with fundamental
dominance; restricted and realistic adequacy; fundamental
majority and its relation with efficiency and fundamental
efficiency; extremal majorities and general ranking principles; the comparison of inequalities in ordinal fundamental
utilities; truncations and balanced bitruncation; the relation
between equity and equality of distribution between two
persons; minimal equity and its relation with equality; the
geometry of equity; the properties of the "divide and
choose" game in its diverse states of knowledge and of
divisibility; the relations between justice and equity; the

---

14. Pages 363-67.

case of identical preferences; generalizations, specifications, and meanings of the concept of equity (restricted and realistic equity, fundamental equity, equality of liberty); the relations of these concepts with efficiency, adequacy, fundamental dominance, preference to and for equality, and others; and so on.

This text has three parts. The first presents basic concepts and, in particular, the principle of *equity* and related criteria. The second analyzes the case of the *distribution* of goods (or services, or jobs), and shows the properties of processes that achieve this distribution. The third is concerned with *justice* and the properties labeled *fundamental*. It defines the criteria and finds their properties and the relations among them. Let us emphasize that *the second and third parts can be read independently from one another*, and that only sections A, B, and C of the first part can be useful to the reading of the third.

I CONCEPTS AND PROBLEMS

A Basic Concepts

1 Personal Situation

A person's situation presents a certain number of traits, all terms that may have to be understood in the broadest possible manner. It can even be described and completely defined, for any specified purpose, by a set of traits. A trait itself has a *nature* that defines it and a *specification* in a given particular situation.

The traits of a personal situation that may have to be considered are, a priori, innumerable: for example (quoted by chance), quantity of a good owned or consumed, income, wealth, aspects of working or living conditions, family situation, social situation or relation, age, sex, physical or psychic characteristics, aspects of health or of type and content of past education or experience, and so on.

Let x be a set of traits of a person. When the specifications of these traits vary, x describes a set X. For example, formally, x can be a set of m parameters (scalars) of given values, and X is the m-dimensional Euclidian space.[1]

2 State of Society

A *society* is a set S of n *persons* represented by the indices i. (All the indices that appear below represent persons who belong to S.)

---

1. A set of traits can always be represented in this way—see *L'Etat et le système des prix* (éd. Dunod, Paris, 1969), second part, chap. 1, and *Le service des masses* (éd. Dunod, Paris, 1970), chap. 11.

For a given problem, an X is defined. In a *state of society*, the x of person i has the specification $x_i \in X$. The set of traits of a personal situation will be defined in a manner sufficiently exhaustive so that the x_i include all the variables of the problem. Then a state of society can be completely represented for all relevant purposes, and thereby can be defined, by the set of the x_i of its members, in other words by the n-tuple

$$\xi = \{x_1, x_2, ..., x_n\}$$

an element of the cartesian product set of the n different X, X^n:

$$\xi \in X^n.$$

3 Permuted States

Two states of society $\xi = \{x_1, ..., x_n\}$ and $\xi' = \{x_1', ..., x_n'\}$ are said to be *permuted* from one another if the two ordered series

$$x_1, ..., x_n$$

and

$$x_1', ..., x_n'$$

are permutations of each other.[2] The significance of these permutations will become apparent when we define equity.

Of course, a permuted state of a possible state may not, in reality, be possible. This depends on the set of traits being considered (consequently, on the definition of x), on the permutation considered, and on the domain of possible states.

4 Domain of Possible States and Constraints

In a given problem, the set of the possible ξ is P, with $P \subset X^n$. Let us note that consideration of P enables one to justify that the same X holds for each i: One can always take a set of personal traits for x that is complete enough to include all the relevant traits for each i; and if x_i for different i have effective possibility domains that are different subsets of X, we include these limitations in P so that we can, a priori, take the same X for all the i. But this last process gives a P that is not symmetric in the sense below.

We say that a subset of X^n is *symmetric* if it contains all the permuted states of its states. P is therefore symmetric if it is possible to permute the x's of the persons, that is, if

---

2. In all this text, by permutation we mean "without omission or repetition." However, in almost any use that we will make of it, one could also call the permutation of x_1, ..., x_n a set of n elements x'_1, ..., x'_n such that for any $i = 1$, ..., n there exists a j such that $x'_i = x_j$ (which allows repetitions and omissions): one can easily check which properties are valid with this definition (for example, the definitions of equity and adequacy).

any permuted state of a possible state is possible. Whether P is symmetric in reality depends on the problem studied with the set of traits of the personal situation which is considered (that is, the definition of x) in the society in question.

When x is a set of parameters, P is in general given by a set of constraints.

A certain set of constraints, which could be only one constraint, is said to be symmetric if the set of the states that satisfy the set of constraints is symmetric. This means that if a state satisfies the set of constraints, the same is true for all its permuted states.

The intersection of symmetric subsets of X^n obviously is symmetric. In particular, the intersection of sets (of states) each defined as satisfying a symmetric set of constraints is symmetric. Thus, the union of symmetric sets of constraints is a symmetric set of constraints.

In particular, if P is defined by such a union, that is, it is the intersection of the sets of states respecting each of these symmetric sets of constraints, it is symmetric. Here are some examples of these constraints. Let y be a parameter of x.

If y is a quantity of a commodity that the members of S consume privatively, and of which they share the total quantity Y, we have

$$\Sigma y_i = Y.$$

This constraint is symmetric.

If y is a common concern for the members of S, for example a quantity of a public good, we have the constraints that this concern for each i, named y_i, is identical to y, and thus is the same for all i (or, for the quantity of a public good that has the nature of an availability for individual uses in quantities y_i, $y_i \leq y$ for all i). This parameter does not change (or this inequality remains valid) in a permutation among the x_i of a possible state. This set of constraints is symmetric.

y also can be a parameter the level of which for each person i is imposed (for example, the age of an individual at a given moment). If these levels are the same for all members of S, this set of constraints is symmetric. If on the other hand, these levels are different for certain members of S, permutation among their x_i is impossible, and this set of constraints is not symmetric.

5 Personal Preferences

People have tastes, opinions, desires, etc., that we may represent by individual preference orderings on states of society. The set of retained traits—and thus x—will be defined in a manner sufficiently exhaustive so that x_i describes all the traits of the society that concern individual i, and so the preference ordering of individual i has as its object various realizations of x_i.[3] Let us utilize

---

3. An individual i may feel concern for the situation of another, i', for various reasons: ordinary physical external effects, but also "social" sentiments or feelings such as altruism, benevolence, malevolence, compassion, love, hate, various sentiments of justice, envy, jealousy, sentiments of inferiority or of superiority, sentiments about conformity or distinction, conformity or violation of certain norms, etc. There are

the classic notations $\underset{i}{\succ}$ (preferred by i), $\underset{i}{\sim}$ (equivalent for i), and $\underset{i}{\succsim}$ ($\underset{i}{\succ}$ or $\underset{i}{\sim}$). Transitivity ($a \succsim b$ and $b \succ c$ implies $a \succ c$, $a \overset{i}{\succ} b$ and $b \succsim c$ implies $a \succ c$, $a \sim b$ and $b \sim c$ implies $a \sim c$) expresses the notion that people are "rational" in the economists' sense.

When the preference ordering of individual i can be represented by an ordinal utility index, we denote this by $u_i(x_i)$.

---

three manners of taking this into account. (1) Persons' preferences can be expressed on ξ; for instance, the property of *equity* described below will then be that ξ is unanimously preferred or indifferent to all its permuted states (or possible permuted states): $\xi \underset{i}{\succsim} \xi^\pi$ for all i and all permuted states ξ^π of ξ (or only possible ones). (2) Sometimes the possibilities are such that when x_i is given, this determines what $x_{i'}$ is for person i'; then i's preferences about $x_{i'}$ can be described within her preferences about x_i; in particular, this will be the case for the two person distribution problem analyzed below. (3) The traits of i' that concern i can be considered not as attributes of i' defined by her name or civil status, but by their objective characteristics. For example, individual i will not be interested in the income of individual i', but in the income of persons of a certain age, having a certain life style, living at a certain place, having a certain family relationship with i, etc., all these traits belonging to i'. This, in addition, helps us to understand the causes of concerns for others in a way that is more meaningful than the *"parce que c'était lui, parce que c'était moi"* (because it was him, because it was me) by which Montaigne "explains" his friendship for La Boétie.

B Efficiency, Equity, Equality

1 Efficiency

The definition of efficiency comes from the domain of possible states and from personal preferences. An efficient state ("Pareto-optimal" or, better, "maximal for unanimity") is a possible state such that there is no other possible state that at least one member of the society prefers and that no member of the society judges to be less desirable. Formally, ξ is efficient if $\xi \in P$ and if there exists no $\xi' \in P$ such that $x'_i \succsim_i x_i$ for any i and $x'_i \succ_i x_i$ for at least one i.

Thus, if a possible state is not efficient, there exists at least one other possible state that is judged better or equivalent by all members of the considered society and that is preferred by at least one of them. It results that if only the members of this society have a voice in the matter (which is necessarily the case if the considered society includes all existing persons), and if their preferences describe their synthetic view for all reasons, the optimum—no matter its definition—is likely to have to be an efficient state, since if state ξ is inefficient, there exists a state ξ' such that the idea that ξ is better than ξ' does not exist in society (while the view that it is worse exists).

2 Equity

A state of society is called equitable if *each person prefers to be in her own situation rather than in any other person's situation*, that is, if each thinks of everyone else: "I'd rather be in my place than in hers." We will add the possibility of indifference to this preference. In other words, equity implies that *no one can be jealous of anyone else*; there is equity when *no one has a possible reason to be envious*. But, of course, there can be nonequity and neither envy nor jealousy because the persons who could experience these sentiments are not prone to them in this state. This equity is defined for a set of traits of the personal situation (x) of which one envisions permutation, and generally for a society S in which the members mutually compare their situations.

Formally, ξ is equitable if

$$x_i \underset{i}{\overset{\succ}{\sim}} x_{i'}$$

for all pairs of individuals i, i'.

Clearly, *a state is equitable if and only if it is unanimously preferred or equivalent to all its permuted states.*

If the preference orderings of these individuals can be represented by ordinal utility indices, equity is defined by

$$u_i(x_i) \geq u_i(x_{i'})$$

for all pairs of persons i, i'. Note that one can always define equity in this manner because the number of persons and thus the number of x_i and $x_{i'}$ is finite, and, therefore, one can always represent a preference between these x_i by a utility index.

But a possible state can have impossible permuted states, if P is not symmetric. This leads to the following concept of *realistic equity*. A state is *realistically equitable* if it is *possible and unanimously preferred or equivalent to all its possible permuted states*. (It of course always holds if no permutation is possible.) If P is symmetric, realistic equity is identical to possible equity. Other variations of the idea of realistic equity are sometimes relevant, such as no person prefers the situation of any other that she can have (for example, jobs that she can perform, and unchangeable and relevant personal parameters have to be the same), or no one wishes to permute her situation with that of any other if this pairwise permutation is possible, with specification of what can occur to the nonmentioned individual situations if this makes a difference. The relations among these variants are easily derived.

If x is such that the individuals choose their own x_i in identical domains of choice, the outcome is obviously equitable (each individual i could have chosen x_j for any j but she preferred x_i). Conversely, if ξ is equitable, it can be obtained by the free choice of her own x_i by each individual in identical domains of choice (these possible domains are those that contain all the x_i of ξ plus any individual situations x that no individual i prefers to her own x_i). Equity thus amounts to equality of liberty in this sense. This property keeps a certain ethical meaningfulness when this choice is considered as notional rather than actual (hence in particular when it is not possible).

The concept of equity obviously is extremely interesting on a strictly *normative* ground both for its direct meaning and for the foregoing property. But the latter property, in its strict sense, requires that the x_i are transferable. With more extended definitions of x, on the contrary, we will see that the concept of equity becomes the ethically more encompassing concept of eudemonistic justice when the set of traits of the personal situation considered (x) becomes very complete.

Realistic equity, where each weakly prefers her situation to that of each other for possible permutations, is a property particularly conducive to *social peace*. This requires that the set of x does not omit relevant traits that can be permuted, that P does not include constraints that can be removed (for example, a law established by certain members of the society), and that individuals are not too mistaken about P and about their own preferences (for example, concerning their capacity to take the place of another and concerning the pleasure that they would find there).

The fact that equity precludes envy and jealousy is valuable in itself, since an absence of these sentiments doubtlessly improves the quality of society (at least for the strong envy verging on jealousy that is the most common use of the term, and other things being equal, since, on the other hand, envy and jealousy can spur not only hostile acts but also competition, productivity and other actions that can have positive effects). Then, if education and suasion do not suffice to restrain or suppress these antisocial sentiments, a recourse to an equitable state or allocation may be commended. Note that what is considered unfavorably are these sentiments, and not only the propensity to have such feelings. It should also be remarked that jealousy requires that one could have what one is jealous of, whereas that is not necessary for envy. Hence jealousy can be prevented by actual impossibility (a property of the set P) and not only by preferring one's own situation or by having a "pure heart." Furthermore, jealousy and morally objectionable envy entail disagreeable sentiments for the person who experiences them (and a variety of possible sentiments for others). The corresponding consumption externality (whereby the person's preferences, satisfaction, or utility also bear on, or are influenced by, others' situations) can be considered as implicitly taken care of in the analyses concerning divisions between two persons carried out below, and its explicit consideration shows that it does not affect the other results, because equity precludes these sentiments and they are disagreeable ones. This externality and its consequences for optimal taxation are analyzed in another study.[4]

In *minimal equity*, for each individual i there exists (at least) one other individual $i' \neq i$ such that $x_i \mathrel{\underset{i}{\succsim}} x_{i'}$ (or $x_i \mathrel{\underset{i}{\succ}} x_{i'}$ for *strict minimal equity*). That is, each individual i does not feel the "last one" (or one of the "last ones") according to her evaluation of the situations. In *realistic minimal equity* (or *realistic strict minimal equity*) these relations hold for at least one $x_{i'}$ that individual i can have instead of x_i, where "can have" is given one of the interpretations noted above (strictly understood, with a possible permutation, with a possible permutation between i and i', etc.).

Restricted equity and restricted minimal equity generalize the realistic concepts in restricting otherwise the comparisons, notably in restricting them to any subset of the permutations.

---

4. See "The Taxation of Conspicuous Consumption," *Revue d'Economie Politique* (forthcoming).

3 Existence and Compatibility

A possible equitable state may not exist: equity may be impossible, or the possible may be necessarily inequitable. If there exist possible equitable states, it may be that none of them is efficient: for each possible equitable state there may exist another possible state that is unanimously preferred. Then, no efficient state is equitable; all equitable states are inefficient and all efficient states are inequitable, i.e., equity is inefficient and efficiency inequitable.

The following problems are therefore posed. Do possible equitable states exist? Do equitable efficient states exist? Do efficient and realistically equitable states exist? Since an efficient state is by definition possible and a possible equitable state is realistically equitable, a positive response to the second question answers positively the other two, and a negative response to the second question is implied by a negative response to either of the other two. The answer to these questions depends on the set of traits of the personal situation retained, the society considered, the preferences of its members, and the domain of possible states, P.

4 Equality

A state of society is called *equal* when all the members have the same personal situation. We therefore can write

$$x_1 = x_2 = \dots = x_n.$$

An equal state is its own permuted state.

An equal state is equitable.

An equal possible state is realistically equitable.

But an equal state can be impossible, and there may very well exist no possible equal state. Similarly, there may or may not exist efficient equal states. (If one exists, it is also possible). These existences depend on the set of traits retained, on the society considered and on the domain of possible states, and, when efficiency is considered, on the preferences of the members of this society.

Equality is useful for several reasons:

- It is rational if the equal items constitute the end values of the ethical judgment;
- It will be used in a proof of the existence of equitable efficient states;
- In one important particular case we will find that the equitable, efficient state is equal;
- Equality often is deemed "natural" (certainly because of the intuition of its rationality), and as a consequence it is often accepted by all, as
  - the starting point in a bargaining process,
  - the reference state in an arbitration,
  - the state-of-threat during a bargaining controlled by an arbiter, that is, the state that will be implemented if the parties do not reach some other agreement (they must then believe it to be possible).

These last uses require that one of the equal states distinguishes itself from the others. This is the case in the problems of distribution studied below, in which one of the possible equal states is unanimously preferred to all others. In these uses of an equal state, the state finally realized must be unanimously preferred to it (with possible indifferences). If none of the other possible states has this characteristic, this equal state is efficient; and we know already that it is equitable. If, on the other hand, there exist possible states unanimously preferred to this equal state, and if this state is used as a threat state in bargaining or as a reference state in an arbitration, it is interesting to know if the unanimously preferred states are or can be equitable, efficient, or both.

C Particular Structures

1 Identical Preferences

The case in which all persons in the society under consideration have identical preference orderings on the useful domain may, a priori, seem fortuitous. This depends both on the society chosen, which may be composed of individuals selected in accordance with a criterion correlated with their preferences, and on the set of traits (of the personal situation) of which one considers the variation. Identical preferences obtain when this set is either properly restricted, or, on the contrary, extremely broad.

The first case, in which the set is restricted, is very easy to see. It is sufficient, for example, that x be reduced to a quantity of a good of which all the members of the society under consideration want to have more. Or, slightly more generally, it is sufficient that x be reduced to a single parameter that all these persons prefer to be larger or smaller. This case presents itself in a more interesting way when there is such a parameter, but instead of the parameter constituting x, x is a set of parameters which determines the first and does not otherwise affect preferences. Then, x has several dimensions and the preferences of the members of the society are identical. If, for example, x is a set of quantities of inputs which produce as an output the quantity of a desired good, the indifference sets are the *isoquants* of this production, for all these people.

Another example of this first case is the one in which x consists of two parameters, one being money received or given up by the person and the other describing a property (possibly but not necessarily a quantity of a good) which is harmful or beneficial only by its *pecuniary effects* (for instance, because it causes loss or profit, or because it corresponds to goods that are bought or sold).

The second case of identical preferences has fundamental importance. It is the case in which the preference orderings describe interpersonally ordinally comparable levels of satisfaction or happiness (rather than only preferences "revealed by choices"), and all the possible causes of differences among satisfactions of the members of the society are included within the variable traits of the personal situations (that is, in the definition of x), and so the corresponding preference orderings (of these x) are in fact the same one. We will later call such a preference ordering the *fundamental preferences* in the society.

When the preferences are identical, we denote the relations of preference and indifference as $\succ$ and $\sim$.

In this case, in an equitable state we must have, for all pairs of persons, i and i', both

$$x_i \succsim x_{i'}$$

and

$$x_{i'} \succsim x_i.$$

We have, thus,

$$x_i \sim x_{i'}.$$

Conversely, if this property holds for each pair i and i', the state is equitable. We therefore have the following result.

Property.

A state is equitable with identical preferences if and only if the x_i all belong to the same indifference class.

2 Problems of the Two Person Society

The case of societies composed of only two persons ($n = 2$) merits special study for several reasons. First, these societies are very common and have their own problems. Second, it is the simplest form of society in number of persons, and this may enable one to obtain results that will suggest other results for larger societies. Finally, many properties of larger societies are composed, in some way, of the analogous properties between members of the society considered two at a time, or are defined from pairs of groups acting as if they were persons. Thus:

- A state of a society is *equitable* if and only if it is equitable for each pair of its members,
- A state of a society is *equal* if and only if it is equal for each pair of its members,
- If a state of a society is *efficient*, it is efficient for each pair of its members when the situation of all others is given,
- The processes of market exchange are processes among transactors considered two at a time,
- We will thoroughly study an important process between two persons, that process in which one of them forms two lots that the other distributes between them,

-    Game theory is particularly developed for two
     persons, and the theory of "*n* person games" uses
     the concepts of the two person case, taking a set of
     players and its complement ("characteristic func-
     tion").

3 Satiety and Satiation

Certain properties of the preferences, which will have to be
considered later, are defined here. These concern transitive
preferences (thus represented by an order)[5] expressed on
sets of quantities of commodities. In measuring each of
these quantities as a dimension of a vector space, each of
these sets is represented by a point in that space. In all this
text, quantities will be assumed to be perfectly divisible
unless the contrary is expressly mentioned. The following
distinctions intuitively imply that "satiety" is being satiated
whereas "satiation" is becoming it.

There is *nonsatiety* for a commodity at a point if a little
larger quantity of this commodity is preferred, the quantities of the other goods remaining constant. There is
nonsatiety of preferences if there is nonsatiety for all
commodities in all points of the useful domain.

We say that there is a *satiation* of preferences if the set
of points preferred or equivalent to one of them is convex.
If these preferences are representable by a utility function,

---

5. *Translator's note*: See the definitions in part III: This text uses the
terms "order" and "strict order" for what is also sometimes called
"preorder" and "order," respectively.

that function is quasiconcave.[6] The term satiation indicates the psychological and economic reason for this property and is therefore preferable to the mathematical term. We say that there is *strict satiation at a point* if there does not exist a *straight line segment* containing this point *in its interior* and made up of points *equivalent* to the former. We say there is *strict satiation* if there is strict satiation at all points of the relevant domain.

---

6. *Translator's note*: A function u: $\mathbb{R}^k \to \mathbb{R}$ is quasiconcave *if* $\{x: u(x) \geq r\}$ is convex for all r. That is, a utility function is quasiconcave if the set of points x, such that the utility index $u(x) \geq r$, is convex for all r.

D Processes

1 Processes and Implementation

More important than determining the existence, and even the properties, of states of society endowed with interesting qualities, is knowing how to implement them. In addition, the definition of a process leading to a desired state is often more simple than the characterization or the simple description of this state. Thus, we can, for example, economize information concerning preferences or possibilities. The most famous example of this is that if one wants an efficient allocation of economic commodities it is sufficient to allow a perfect market to function. We have also remarked that individuals' choices in identical domains implement an equitable allocation of the chosen objects. These two cases coexist if the perfect market is one with equal incomes (identical budget sets). Generally, the definition of a process is a "rule of the game," or a "constitution." It would be interesting to know other processes that implement equity.

Conforming to tradition in economics, processes will be valued only by the states they achieve, and judged only according to properties of these states. These judgments omit several things: the costs of realization (time, transferring, evaluating and processing of information, etc.), the socio-psychological effects of the procedure[7] (one may, for

---

7. *Author's note of 1997*: These aspects of processes, their analysis and evaluation, and the consideration of individuals' preferences about them, constitute the central topic of the book *La bonne économie (la réciprocité générale)* (Presses Universitaires de France, Paris, 1984).

example, deplore that competition is based on egoism and hostility among men, and fear that it favors these distasteful attitudes, but at the same time realize that it may assure social efficiency of the economy), and the ethical values of the processes *per se*—which are, however, implicitly acknowledged in the following reasonings.

2 Free Exchange

The central subject of classical political economy is precisely a process: *free exchange*. Its qualities of *efficiency* can be considered as the principal "discovery" of this discipline. It therefore will be of interest to note that this process also has certain qualities from the point of view of (end-result) *social justice* which are properties of *equity*.

The classical exchange is the exchange of private goods between persons two at a time: each exchange is *bilateral*. *Free* means here that each person has the right to abstain from exchange: each of the two participants in an exchange has a right of *veto* on the act. An *exchange system* is a set of exchanges among the members of a society, and a *perfect market* is an exchange system performed with a system of prices that are nondiscriminatory (with respect to quantities and to persons),[8] parametric (that is, given to each individual), and market equilibrating (that is, the quantities supplied and demanded of each good are equal). Classical *perfect competition* is a special case of perfect market (Lange-Lerner socialism is another example).

---

8. Cf. *L'Etat et le système des prix*, op. cit., second part.

The quality related to "efficiency" of free exchange results from its definition: if there is exchange, each person prefers the state with exchange to the state without it, since each person had the opportunity to abstain (with the possibility of indifference if the exchange requires no effort or transaction cost). In addition, a prominent result of economics is that the perfect market is efficient in the precise sense defined above ("Pareto optimality" or maximality for unanimity). This applies in particular to perfect competition.

The property of equity of free exchange will appear when we use as the set of traits of personal situations, x, the set of quantities exchanged by the person. In other words, these persons are then considered solely as exchangers. All the other traits of their situations are counted among the parameters that form their preferences. This is in particular the case of the initial quantities of goods and resources with which they are endowed before exchange. We will count the quantities acquired by a person positively, and the quantities given up negatively. When the properties of equity of free exchange or trade are enunciated without further qualification, it will be understood that it is with this set of traits x.

3 Forming and Assigning Lots

Other processes may possess properties of equity.

In the two person case, a certain tradition holds that the process whereby one person forms two lots (personal situations), and the second chooses between them, leaving the remaining one to the first person, assures a certain "equity" (in order for this process to have meaning, it obviously is necessary that each of the lots can be attributed to each of the persons). And, in fact, this process guarantees at least that the second person prefers her lot to that of the first (or be indifferent between them). But for the resulting state to be equitable, the first person also should prefer her lot to that of the other (or be indifferent between them). Now, that is not necessarily the case; it depends on the form of the domain of possible states, as can be seen in the following example.

The lots are the quantities x_1 and x_2 of a commodity. The preference of each of the persons is only to receive for herself the largest quantity possible. Consequently, the definition of equity, that

$$x_1 \mathrel{\underset{1}{\succsim}} x_2$$

and

$$x_2 \mathrel{\underset{2}{\succsim}} x_1,$$

amounts to

$$x_1 \geq x_2$$

and

$$x_2 \geq x_1,$$

that is,

$$x_1 = x_2.$$

Equity and equality in this case are the same property. Figure 1 depicts the problem in the plane of coordinates x_1 and x_2. The first bisector of the axes is the locus of equal states, and therefore also the locus of equitable states. The hypothesis that for all the possible solutions each lot can be attributed to each individual means that if $x_1 = x'$ and $x_2 = x''$ is possible, then $x_1 = x''$ and $x_2 = x'$ is also possible; that is, if a point (x_1, x_2) is possible, the point that is symmetric to it with respect to the first bisector of the axes also is possible. The domain of possible states, P (the shaded area), therefore is assumed to be symmetric with respect to this line. Figure 1a represents the case of the

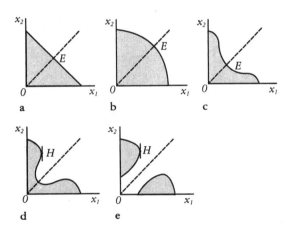

Figure 1

division of a given quantity X between x_1 and x_2, P being then defined by $x_1 + x_2 \leq X$ (perhaps, in addition to $x_1 \geq 0$ and $x_2 \geq 0$—cf. infra the discussion of this point). Figures 1b, 1c, 1d, and 1e represent other forms of P.

If the first person forms the lots and the second chooses, then, when the first has fixed two quantities x' and x'', the second person takes the larger and leaves the smaller to the first, that is, leaves $\text{Min}[x', x'']$. The first person therefore chooses a pair (x', x'') that makes this quantity as large as possible. The state realized therefore is defined by the following relation, which describes the behavior of the first person:

$$\underset{(x', x'') \in P}{\text{Max}} \ \text{Min} \ [x', x''],$$

where x' and x'' are the coordinates of a point of the plane; and by the following attribution due to the second person:

$$x_2 = \text{Max}[x', x''], \ x_1 = \text{Min}[x', x''].$$

In the cases of figures 1a, 1b, and 1c, the result is the efficient equal state E: the process therefore is *equitable, efficient, and equal*, and *it makes no difference whether one is the person who forms the lots or the one who assigns them*. In the case of figure 1d, in which all the equal states are inefficient, and in the case of figure 1e, in which all the equal states are impossible, the result is H—which represents an efficient state in which $x_1 < x_2$. The process in these cases therefore is *efficient* but *inequitable* and *unequal*, and *it is better to be the one who assigns the lots than the one who forms them.* (This state is what we will call in the third part *practically just.*)

In contrast, in the case of *distribution problems*, studied below and of which the division of a commodity is a special case, we will see that this process—called "divide and choose"—is *equitable*, but that it is in general inefficient and unequal, and such that *it is better to be the one who forms the lots than the one who assigns them.*

E Distribution Problems

1 Constraints

A distribution problem consists of dividing a set of given quantities of commodities among members of a society. The given quantities will be called resources, and the bundle of quantities received by a person will be called a *lot*. Let us specify that these commodities are private goods for these persons, that these persons care only about their own lots and not about those of others (no externality in this society for this problem), and that each person prefers to have more of each commodity (nonsatiety).

Let m be the number of commodities and $j = 1, 2, ..., m$ the index of the commodities.

Let x_i^j denote the quantity of commodity j allotted to person i.

x_i is the lot of person i and it is the bundle of the x_i^j for this i. It therefore is the vector of these quantities. X then is the Euclidian m-dimensional space $\mathbb{R}^m$.

Let x^j be the total given quantity (resource) of commodity j. Let us denote the vector of the x^j as X. P is defined by the set of *distribution constraints*

$$\sum_i x_i^j = x^j$$

or

$$\sum x_i = X.$$

Equality in these relations means that all the resources are distributed to the members of the society. If it could be otherwise, equality would be replaced with inequality $\leq$ in these constraints. But nonsatiety requires as a necessary condition of efficiency that equality be achieved. For all practical purposes it is sufficient to consider these constraints using an equal sign.

Moreover, strict interpretation of the problem seems to imply that $x_i^j \geq 0$ for all i and j, and $x^j > 0$ for all j. In many applications we will have these constraints. But if we refer to $x_i^j < 0$ as the quantity $|x_i^j|$ of the commodity j *given up* by person i, then we may have the same problem without constraints on the sign of x_i^j for some j's or for all j, possibly depending on i. Similarly, $x^j < 0$ means that the quantity $|x^j|$ of commodity j must be given up by the considered society. When for a j the x_i^j may be of any sign, then the "resource" x^j may be of any sign, and it may in particular be $x^j = 0$ (meaning that commodity j is transferred between members of the society). For certain j's, in fact, the constraints $x_i^j \leq 0$ and $x^j \leq 0$ are required (for example, if it is labor—or another factor—that all the members of the society can produce but not use). In all that follows, the x_i^j and x^j can have any sign, or they can be subject to these constraints of sign, provided that for each j the constraint is the same for all i. This last condition ensures that the set of constraints for each j is symmetric. Note that it does not exclude the important case where a commodity j is the specific labor of some person i, since, then, we would describe this person's working for others as the allocation of a given total duration of her time between this labor and her own use of it as leisure or work for herself.

More generally, the x_i^j can be subject to constraints of the form

$$\underline{\xi}^j \leq x_i^j \leq \overline{\xi}^j,$$

where $\underline{\xi}^j$ and $\overline{\xi}^j$ are given constants,[9] on condition that, for each j, the x_i^j for all i are subject to the same constraints. This set of constraints therefore is symmetric. As special cases, we may have $\underline{\xi}^j = 0$, or $\overline{\xi}^j = 0$, or $\underline{\xi}^j = -\infty$, or $\overline{\xi}^j = +\infty$. The boundaries, moreover, must be subject to the condition

$$n\underline{\xi}^j \leq x^j \leq n\overline{\xi}^j,$$

so that

$$\underline{\xi}^j \leq g^j \leq \overline{\xi}^j,$$

where

$$g^j = \frac{x^j}{n}.$$

The set P defined by these constraints is symmetric.

2 Properties

Whatever the sign of the x_i^j, we still assume that each person cares only about her own lot and not about those of

---

9. Hereafter the symbol ξ will cease to have the meaning it had in sections A and B.

others (with a qualification introduced below for $n = 2$). If person i gives up a piece of commodity j, nonsatiety is evidenced by the fact that she prefers to give up less of it, that is, given the $x_i^{j'}$ for the $j' \neq j$, she prefers $|x_i^j|$ to be smaller and, thus, x_i^j (which is negative) to be larger. This last form of the property therefore is the same whatever the sign of x_i^j.

The problems of distribution are specified according to the number of persons n, the number of commodities m, the resources, the possibilities of negativity, and the structure of the preferences of these persons for these commodities. Two specific cases of distribution problems are the exchange problems and the division problems defined below. We call an equitable or efficient or equal distribution (or exchange or division) a state of society which is *possible* and, respectively, equitable or efficient or equal for a distribution (or exchange or division) problem.

There is only one *equal distribution* when the distribution constraints are with equal signs: the one in which each commodity is equally divided among all the persons. Calling

$$g = \frac{X}{n}$$

the vector of the g^j, the equal distribution is that in which

$$x_i = g$$

for all i. If the distribution constraints are with inequality, the equal distributions would have been all those in which each person i receives the same $x_i = x$, subject to the vector

An *exchange problem* is a distribution problem in which $x^j = 0$ for all j, that is, $\sum_i x_i^j = 0$ for all j, or $\sum x_i = 0$, or $X = 0$.[12] One must not confuse exchange, thus defined, which is a *problem*, with the free exchange considered above, which is a process. In an exchange, $g^j = 0$ for all j, or $g = 0$. That is, "equal exchange" is the *state without effective exchange*; its interest as a state of reference or of threat is particularly clear in this case; in particular, the socially interesting properties of the end-result of free exchange result from the fact that each party utilizes the state without exchange as a threat.

When there is only one commodity ($m = 1$), a distribution of resources is a division of this commodity and the distribution problem is a *division problem*. Any division is efficient. x_i and $x_{i'}$ being the quantities of the commodity allocated to persons i and i', the expressions

$$x_i \underset{i}{\gtrsim} x_{i'}$$

and

$$x_{i'} \underset{i'}{\gtrsim} x_i$$

are, respectively, equivalent to the expressions

$$x_i \geq x_{i'}$$

---

12. *Translator's note*: Here we conceive of x_i as representing amounts exchanged, rather than as representing amounts possessed.

and

$$x_{i'} \geq x_i \,,$$

and their set is identical to $x_i = x_{i'}$. There exists, therefore, one and only one equitable division: the *equal division* in which each of the *n* persons receives the same fraction *g* of the total quantity *X*.

4 Questions

In the general case, there of course always exists an equitable distribution: the equal distribution. But, when *m* > 1, *the equal distribution is no longer in general neither the only equitable distribution nor an efficient distribution.* If the equal distribution is not efficient, there exist distributions, and notably efficient distributions, that are unanimously preferred to the equal distribution. But are they also equitable, or are any of them equitable?

The following questions are thus posed. For any society, or for two persons, or for a society with identical preferences,

- Do there exist equitable and efficient distributions, what are their properties, how large is their set?
- Is there a relation between equity and unanimous preference to the equal distribution?
- Is there a relation between these properties and, in addition, efficiency?
- What is a process "divide and choose" worth with respect to equity, to efficiency, to preference to

equal distribution, and to the relative advantage of
the two roles, in the various cases of information,
divisibilities, and specific rules?
- What are free exchange processes worth with
respect to equity?

The second part answers these questions and others and
shows the properties of the structures and processes of
distribution. Nonsatiety and satiation keep being assumed.
But the results are specified according to whether or not
this satiation is strict. More precisely, in most of the
problems the two cases are: one, that in which the preferences are subject to no condition other than nonsatiety and
satiation; and, two, that in which they are subject to the
sole additional condition that their satiation be strict in a
single state, the equal distribution (we say then that there is
strict satiation at equality). Of course, this last structure
holds in particular if satiation is everywhere strict.

Some of the main properties obtained appears in the
following results for the distribution of divisible goods. A
restriction on satiation necessary for the results to be true
is indicated in parentheses; when nothing is indicated, there
is no restriction. The second part also proves other related
results obtained with other structures of satiation, information, divisibility, etc., and it studies the properties of a
few other phenomena concerning the same issues.

5 Some Results on Equity in Distributions

a The Two Person Case

Lemma 1
(1) *If a person prefers a distribution to equality, she prefers her lot to that of the other in this distribution.*
(2) The same holds if "prefers" is replaced with "prefers or is indifferent to."

Theorem 1
(1) *Any distribution unanimously preferred to equality is equitable.*
(2) The same holds with "unanimously preferred or equivalent."

Corollaries
(1) Any efficient distribution unanimously preferred (or equivalent) to equality is efficient and equitable.
(2) There exist distributions that are equitable, efficient and unanimously preferred or equivalent to equality. That is, at least one exists, and if only one exists it is equality.
(3) *There exist distributions that are both equitable and efficient.* That is, at least one exists, and if only one exists it is equality.

Theorem 2 (Strict)
A process of "divide and choose" with perfect information and divisibility and standard rules,
(1) *is equitable*;
except in the case in which it yields equality,

(2) *the process is better than equality for the divider and worse than equality for the chooser, and it is better to divide than to choose,*
(3) *it is inefficient.*

Theorem 3
Bilateral free exchange is equitable.

b The General Case

Theorem 4
There exist distributions (at least one) that are equitable, efficient and unanimously preferred or equivalent to equality.

Theorem 4'
A perfect market is equitable with respect to exchanges.

Corollaries
With respect to exchanges,
(1) a perfect market is efficient and equitable,
(2) perfect competition is equitable,
(3) perfect competition is efficient and equitable.

Lemma 2
(1) *If a person prefers a distribution to equality, she prefers her lot to that of at least one other person in this distribution.*
(2) The same holds if "prefers" is replaced with "prefers or is indifferent to."

Theorem 5
(1) *Any distribution unanimously preferred or equivalent to equality is minimally equitable.*
(2) Any distribution unanimously preferred to equality is strictly minimally equitable.

c The Case of Identical Preferences

Theorem 6
Equality is efficient.

Theorem 7 (Strict at equality)
Equality is unanimously preferred to all other equitable distributions.

Corollary
Equality is the only equitable and efficient distribution.

II DISTRIBUTION

A Two Persons

1 Properties

a Concepts

α Framework

First consider the case in which $n = 2$, with $i = 1$, 2, and $m \geq 2$. The problems are analyzed best in a generalization of the Edgeworth Box in an m-dimensional Euclidian Space, instead of the usual two dimensions. But the case in which $m = 2$ allows graphic representation and the reasoning can be followed with the aid of the figures that appear below that describe it. In an m-dimensional Euclidian space, lines and hypersurfaces are the 1-dimensional and the $m - 1$-dimensional manifolds, respectively. For $m = 3$ and for $m = 2$, the hypersurfaces are surfaces and lines, respectively.

The "generalized Edgeworth Box" is generalized in two ways. First, the number of dimensions of the space may be greater than two. Second, the domain of possible states is not necessarily defined by $x_i^j \geq 0$ for all i and j. The shape of the box is determined by the constraints $\underline{\xi}^j \leq x_i^j \leq \overline{\xi}^j$, discussed above. In particular, certain x_i^j and even x^j may be allowed to be, or may have to be, negative.

In the m-dimensional Euclidian space, from a point O_1, the quantities of one of the m commodities are represented on each of the m axes. Let O_2 be the point such that

$$\overrightarrow{O_1 O_2} = X.$$

A *distribution* is represented by a *point M* such that

$$\overrightarrow{O_1M} = x_1$$

and

$$\overrightarrow{MO_2} = x_2.$$

If, as in the classic Edgeworth Box, the only constraints other than those of distribution were $x_i^j \geq 0$, the generalized Edgeworth Box would be the hyperparallelepiped locus of the points M such that

$$0 \leq \overrightarrow{O_1M} \leq X;$$

for $m = 3$ this would be a parallelepiped, and for $m = 2$ it would be the parallelogram O_1AO_2B of figure 2.

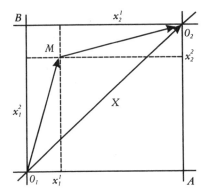

Figure 2

If certain x_i^j can be negative, we will keep the same representation but certain possible M's can then be situated outside this locus. Figure 3 shows the four possible cases for $m = 2$ ($j = 1, 2$). The following are nonnegative (the forbidden zones are hatched): in 3a all the x_i^j, in 3b the two x_i^1, in 3c the two x_i^2, in 3d no x_i^j; furthermore, x^1 could be negative or null in the second and in the last cases, and x^2 could be negative or null in the third and in the last cases.

If, more generally, certain x_1^j and x_2^j are subject to the constraints

$$\underline{\xi}^j \leq x_i^j \leq \bar{\xi}^j \qquad (i = 1, 2),$$

then the condition

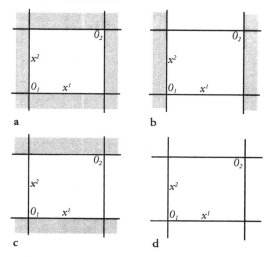

Figure 3

$$x_1^j + x_2^j = x^j$$

shows that the domain of possible states is defined by

$$\underline{\xi}^j \leq x_i^j \leq \overline{\overline{\xi}}^j \quad (i = 1, 2)$$

where

$$\underline{\xi}^j = \text{Max } [\underline{\xi}^j, x^j - \overline{\xi}^j]$$

$$\overline{\overline{\xi}}^j = \text{Min } [\overline{\xi}^j, x^j - \underline{\xi}^j],$$

which implies

$$\underline{\xi}^j + \overline{\overline{\xi}}^j = x^j.$$

Figure 4 shows an example of such a situation for $m = 2$.

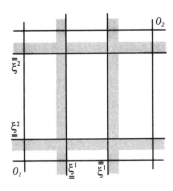

Figure 4

The point representing the *equal distribution* is the midpoint G of the segment $O_1 O_2$ (figure 4). It is such that

$$\overrightarrow{O_1 G} = \overrightarrow{GO_2} = g = \frac{X}{2} = \frac{\overrightarrow{O_1 O_2}}{2}.$$

A *division* of X into two lots ξ and ξ' such that

$$\xi + \xi' = X$$

is represented by a *pair of points M and M' which are symmetric with respect to G* (figure 5), and such that

$$\xi = \overrightarrow{O_1 M} = \overrightarrow{M'O_2}$$

and

$$\xi' = \overrightarrow{O_1 M'} = \overrightarrow{MO_2}.$$

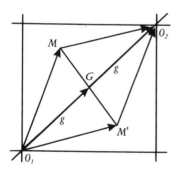

Figure 5

The division (ξ, ξ') can be distributed as two possible distributions, $x_1 = \xi$ and $x_2 = \xi'$ represented by point M, and $x_1 = \xi'$ and $x_2 = \xi$ represented by point M'.

The equal division is represented by G (M and M' coincide).

The indifference hypersurfaces of individual 1, called I_1, are represented in the system of axes that have origin O_1. The indifference hypersurfaces I_2 of individual 2 are represented in the system of axes that have origin O_2, with the axes parallel to those of the preceding system but oriented in the opposite directions (the same good being measured on two parallel axes). For $m = 2$, some of these indifference curves are drawn on figure 6. Call I_1^* and I_2^* the loci of the points representing distributions equivalent to equality for individuals 1 and 2 respectively, that is, the hypersurfaces of I_1 and I_2 passing through G (figure 6).

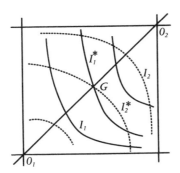

Figure 6

β *Indifferent Divisions*

We will say that a division of X into two lots ξ and ξ' is *indifferent* for a person if this individual is indifferent between ξ and ξ'. That is, this individual is indifferent concerning the assignment of the lots. Indifferent divisions for a person are those for which the two representative points M and M' are on the same indifference hypersurface of that person. Indeed, $\xi \underset{1}{\sim} \xi'$ is written $\overrightarrow{O_1 M} \underset{1}{\sim} \overrightarrow{O_1 M'}$ and $\xi \underset{2}{\sim} \xi'$ is written $\overrightarrow{MO_2} \underset{2}{\sim} \overrightarrow{M'O_2}$.

The loci of the points M, representing the distributions of which the corresponding divisions are indifferent for individual 1 or for individual 2 are *the hypersurfaces of indifferent divisions* for these persons. They are denoted D_1 and D_2, respectively, and they are defined by the following equations where $x_1 + x_2 = X$:

$$D_1 : \ \overrightarrow{O_1 M} \underset{1}{\sim} \overrightarrow{MO_2} \ \text{ or } \ u_1(x_1) = u_1(x_2)$$

$$D_2 : \ \overrightarrow{O_1 M} \underset{2}{\sim} \overrightarrow{MO_2} \ \text{ or } \ u_2(x_2) = u_2(x_1).^{[1]}$$

Certain properties of D_1 and D_2 are obvious. Figure 7 shows D_1 for $m = 2$. We would draw D_2 similarly. First, these hypersurfaces *pass through* G since when M is at this point $\overrightarrow{O_1 M} = \overrightarrow{MO_2}$ and $x_1 = x_2 = g$. Second, each is *symmetric with respect to* G. Indeed, the distribution represent-

---

1. *Translator's note*: The hypersurfaces or surfaces ($m = 3$) or curves ($m = 2$) of equal division are now standardly referred to as Kolm's hypersurfaces, surfaces, or curves (see, for instance, M. Fleurbaey's *Théories Economiques de la Justice* (Economica, Paris, 1996)).

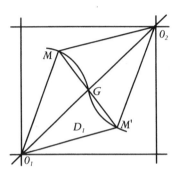

Figure 7

ed by the point M', symmetric to M with respect to G, corresponds to the same division as the distribution represented by M. M and M' are the two distributions of the same single division. Thus, if M is on D_1, M' also is on it. In other words, $\overrightarrow{O_1M} = \overrightarrow{M'O_2}$ and $\overrightarrow{MO_2} = \overrightarrow{O_1M'}$ imply that, for $i = 1$ or 2, $\overrightarrow{O_1M} \underset{i}{\sim} \overrightarrow{MO_2}$ implies $\overrightarrow{O_1M'} \underset{i}{\sim} \overrightarrow{M'O_2}$, that is, M' is on D_i if M is on it. In the case $m = 2$, the fact that each of the curves D_1 and D_2 passes through G and is symmetric with respect to G implies that this point is, for them, an *inflection point*.

The loci D_1 and D_2 can also be built up heuristically. Let us present this construction for D_1—the same can be made for D_2 *mutatis mutandi*. Given an indifference hypersurface I_1 of individual 1, consider the hypersurface I_1' which is symmetric to I_1 with respect to G. I_1 and I_1' intersect on a manifold μ of at most $m - 2$ dimensions. Let M be any point of μ, and M' the point symmetric to M with respect to G. Since M is on I_1, M' is on I_1'. Since M is on I_1', M' is on I_1, the hypersurface that is symmetric to

I_1' with respect to G. Thus M' also is in μ, and consequently μ is symmetric with respect to G. Since M and M'
are on I_1, $\overrightarrow{O_1M} \underset{1}{\sim} \overrightarrow{O_1M'}$. And since M and M' are symmetric with respect to G, $\overrightarrow{O_1M'} = \overrightarrow{MO_2}$ and $\overrightarrow{O_1M} = \overrightarrow{M'O_2}$.
Thus, $\overrightarrow{O_1M} \underset{1}{\sim} \overrightarrow{MO_2}$ and $\overrightarrow{O_1M'} \underset{1}{\sim} \overrightarrow{M'O_2}$. The result of this is
that M and M' are on D_1, and thus μ is on D_1. When the
hypersurface I_1 describes the network of indifference loci of
individual 1, μ describes D_1. In the $m = 2$ case of figure
8, μ consists of two points M and M' which are symmetric
with respect to G.

This construction confirms that D_1 and D_2 are each
symmetric with respect to G and pass through G. This last
property is obtained by considering the indifference
hypersurface passing through G, I_1^* (or I_2^*), for which μ
contains this point (and is even reduced to it in the case of
strict satiation at equality).

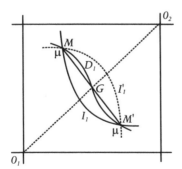

Figure 8

D_1 divides the space into two regions containing, respectively, O_1 and O_2. Let M be a point in the second region, and N a point of D_1 such that $\overrightarrow{MN}$ is parallel to $\overrightarrow{O_1O_2}$ (figure 9). The equality

$$\overrightarrow{O_1M} = \overrightarrow{O_1N} + \overrightarrow{NM}$$

shows that the lot of individual 1, in the distribution represented by M, contains more of all the commodities than does her lot in the distribution represented by N. Similarly,

$$\overrightarrow{NO_2} = \overrightarrow{NM} + \overrightarrow{MO_2}$$

shows that $\overrightarrow{NO_2}$ contains more of all the commodities than $\overrightarrow{MO_2}$. Therefore, and since N is on D_1, we have

$$\overrightarrow{O_1M} \underset{1}{\succ} \overrightarrow{O_1N} \underset{1}{\sim} \overrightarrow{NO_2} \underset{1}{\succ} \overrightarrow{MO_2},$$

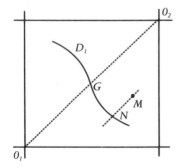

Figure 9

so that

$$\overrightarrow{O_1M} \succsim_1 \overrightarrow{MO_2}.$$

That is, in the distribution represented by M, individual 1 prefers her lot to that of individual 2. It is shown in the same way that the inverse situation prevails on the O_1 side of D_1, and analogous proofs can be provided for individual 2.

Hence, the hypersurface (curve for $m = 2$) D_1 divides the space into two regions: the one that contains O_1, in which individual 1 prefers $\overrightarrow{MO_2}$ to $\overrightarrow{O_1M}$—that is, she prefers the lot of individual 2 to her own; and the one that contains O_2, in which individual 1 prefers $\overrightarrow{O_1M}$ to $\overrightarrow{MO_2}$—that is, she prefers her lot to that of individual 2. Similarly, D_2 divides the space into two regions: the one that contains O_1, in which individual 2 prefers $\overrightarrow{MO_2}$ to $\overrightarrow{O_1M}$—that is, she prefers her lot to that of individual 1; and the one that contains O_2, in which individual 2 prefers $\overrightarrow{O_1M}$ to $\overrightarrow{MO_2}$—that is, she prefers the lot of individual 1 to her own. The locus Q of the points M representing *equitable distributions* is thus the part of the space situated both on the O_2 side of D_1 and on the O_1 side of D_2 (points on D_1 and D_2 are included, and, if necessary, constraints are added on the sign of x_i^j). Figure 10 represents this for $m = 2$. Q is not empty due to the fact that it contains G which is a point on its border.

b Equality and "Jealousy" or "Envy"

Let us now prove lemma 1. We also will see certain other properties that enrich its statement and are obtained when

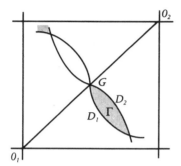

Figure 10

satiation is strict at equality (that is, at G). Three proofs will be presented because the structures that they bring to light are of interest in themselves.

(1) The most direct proof probably is the following. It is given for individual 1, but it may be repeated identically, *mutatis mutandi*, for individual 2.

Let P_1 be the hyperplane tangent to I_1^* at G, if it is unique, and otherwise let it be any one of the hyperplanes passing through G such that I_1^* does not have points on both sides of P_1 (the satiation of individual 1 guarantees its existence). Because of the satiation of individual 1, all the distributions preferred to equality by individual 1 are represented by points situated on the O_2 side of P_1, and all the distributions that are represented by points situated on the O_1 side of P_1 are judged by individual 1 to be inferior to equality.

Now, let M be a point representing a distribution that individual 1 prefers to equality (figure 11), and let M' be symmetric to M with respect to G. M is on the O_2 side of P_1, and, since P_1 passes through G, M' is on the O_1 side of P_1. Consequently, the distribution represented by M' is judged by individual 1 to be inferior to equality. We thus have

$$\overrightarrow{O_1M} \underset{1}{\succ} \overrightarrow{O_1G} \underset{1}{\succ} \overrightarrow{O_1M'}.$$

But

$$\overrightarrow{O_1M'} = \overrightarrow{MO_2}$$

because M and M' are symmetric with respect to G. Thus,

$$\overrightarrow{O_1M} \underset{1}{\succ} \overrightarrow{MO_2}.$$

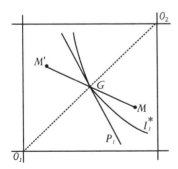

Figure 11

If M now represents a distribution equivalent to equality for individual 1 but different from equality, and if the satiation of individual 1 is strict at equality, the point M' symmetric to M with respect to G is on the O_1 side of I_1^* and consequently individual 1 prefers equality to the distribution represented by M'. We thus have

$$\overrightarrow{O_1M} \underset{1}{\sim} \overrightarrow{O_1G} \underset{1}{\succ} \overrightarrow{O_1M'},$$

and, thus,

$$\overrightarrow{O_1M} \underset{1}{\succ} \overrightarrow{MO_2}.$$

Note that in this case there are two possible situations. In the first (the more "normal") situation, M is not on P_1, M' therefore is not either, and more precisely, M is on the O_2 side of P_1 while M' is on the O_1 side of P_1 (figure 12). In the second situation (figure 13), I_1^* contains the straight line segment GM, and M and M' are on P_1, but M' is nevertheless on the O_1 side of I_1^* because of the definition of strict satiation.

But, if satiation of individual 1 is not strict at equality, there exist points that are symmetric with respect to G and are both located on I_1^*, P_1, and also D_1, as well as all the straight line segment that joins them (figure 14).[2] Then, $\overrightarrow{O_1M} \underset{1}{\sim} \overrightarrow{O_1G}$, which implies that M is not on the O_1 side of P_1, and thus that the symmetric M' to M with respect to G

---

2. *Translator's note*: Note that in figure 14 M' may or may not lie on I_1^*, even when M and M' lie on P_1.

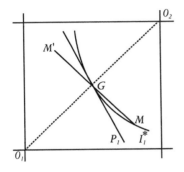

Figure 12

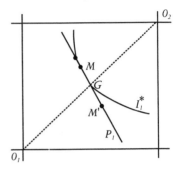

Figure 13

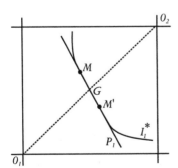

Figure 14

is not on the O_2 side of P_1, assures only that M' is not on the O_2 side of I_1^*, that is, that individual 1 does not prefer the distribution represented by M' to equality or to the distribution represented by M. And

$$\overrightarrow{O_1M} \underset{1}{\sim} \overrightarrow{O_1G} \underset{1}{\succsim} \overrightarrow{O_1M'},$$

implies

$$\overrightarrow{O_1M} \underset{1}{\succsim} \overrightarrow{MO_2}.$$

Thus, the following results hold:

- *If a person prefers a certain distribution to equality, she prefers her lot to that of the other in this distribution.*

- *If a person does not prefer equality to a certain distribution, she does not prefer the lot of the other to her own in this distribution.*

- *If a person prefers the lot of the other to her own in a certain distribution, she prefers equality to this distribution.*

- *If a person does not prefer her lot to that of the other in a certain distribution, she does not prefer this distribution to equality.*

- *If a person with strict satiation at equality does not prefer equality to a certain unequal distribution, she prefers her lot to that of the other in this distribution.*

- *If a person with strict satiation at equality does not prefer her lot to that of the other in a certain unequal distribution, she prefers equality to this distribution.*

(2) These results can also be obtained directly from the elementary properties of satiation (quasiconcavity). Call ξ and ξ' two sets (vectors) of quantities of commodities, and note $\succ$, $\sim$, $\succsim$ for a preference with satiation (not further defined for the moment). The following properties hold, where "strict" means the hypothesis that satiation is strict on at least one point of the segment $\xi\ \xi'$, for example $(\xi + \xi')/2$ or ξ or ξ':

$$\xi' \sim \xi \qquad \Rightarrow \qquad \frac{\xi + \xi'}{2} \succsim \xi. \tag{1}$$

$$\left.\begin{array}{l} \text{strict} \\ \xi' \sim \xi \\ \xi' \neq \xi \end{array}\right\} \qquad \Rightarrow \qquad \frac{\xi + \xi'}{2} \succ \xi. \tag{2}$$

$$\xi' \succ \xi \qquad \Rightarrow \qquad \frac{\xi + \xi'}{2} \succ \xi. \tag{3}$$

Relations (1), and (2) and (3), respectively, give

$$\xi' \succsim \xi \qquad \Rightarrow \qquad \frac{\xi + \xi'}{2} \succsim \xi. \tag{4}$$

$$\left.\begin{array}{l} \text{strict} \\ \xi' \succsim \xi \\ \xi' \neq \xi \end{array}\right\} \qquad \Rightarrow \qquad \frac{\xi + \xi'}{2} \succ \xi. \tag{5}$$

The logical inversion of relations (3), (4), and (5) give, respectively,

$$\xi \gtrsim \frac{\xi + \xi'}{2} \quad \Rightarrow \quad \xi \gtrsim \xi'. \tag{6}$$

$$\xi \succ \frac{\xi + \xi'}{2} \quad \Rightarrow \quad \xi \succ \xi'. \tag{7}$$

$$\left. \begin{array}{l} \text{strict} \\ \xi \gtrsim \frac{\xi + \xi'}{2} \\ \xi \neq \xi' \end{array} \right\} \Rightarrow \quad \xi' \succ \xi. \tag{8}$$

Now, if we call ξ and ξ' the two lots of a distribution, we have

$$\frac{\xi + \xi'}{2} = g = \overrightarrow{O_1 G} = \overrightarrow{GO_2}.$$

Properties (3) to (8) are then the announced results when they are applied respectively to $\xi = x_1$ and $\xi' = x_2$ for the preferences of individual 1, and to $\xi = x_2$ and $\xi' = x_1$ for the preferences of individual 2.

(3) These results can equally well be derived from the heuristic construction of the loci D_1 and D_2 described above.

For example, take D_1. A hypersurface I_1 and the hypersurface symmetric to it with respect to G, I'_1, intersect when I_1 is on the O_1 side of I_1^*, but do not intersect when I_1 is on the O_2 side of I_1^*. The limiting case is the one in which I_1 is I_1^*, and in which μ is reduced to G if the preferences of individual 1 have strict satiation at G. Thus, by this construction the I_1 hypersurfaces situated on the O_2 side of I_1^* do not generate points of D_1. Consequently, there is no point of D_1 on the O_2 side of I_1^*. Thus, neither is there any point of I_1^* situated on the O_1 side of D_1. And all the I_1, other than I_1^*, which give points of D_1 are on the O_1 side of I_1^*. Thus, all the points of D_1 that are not on I_1^* are on the O_1 side of I_1^*, and all the points of I_1^* that are not on D_1 are on the O_2 side of D_1. Finally, D_1 and I_1^* have the point G in common, and if satiation of individual 1 is strict there, they have only this point in common.

Since the hypersurfaces D_1 and I_1^* each lie entirely on one side of the other,[3] and have the point G in common, they are tangent at this point (figure 15).

These results show that if a point M is situated:

- on the O_2 side of I_1^*, it is on the O_2 side of D_1,

- on the O_2 side of I_1^* or on I_1^*, it is on the O_2 side of D_1 or on D_1,

- on the O_1 side of D_1, it is on the O_1 side of I_1^*,

- on the O_1 side of D_1 or on D_1, it is on the O_1 side of I_1^* or on I_1^*,

---

3. *Translator's note*: That is, they do not cross.

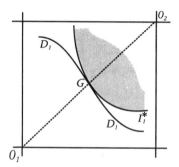

Figure 15

and, with strict satiation of individual 1 at G and an M different from G,

- on the O_2 side of I_1^* or on I_1^*, it is on the O_2 side of D_1, and

- on the O_1 side of D_1 or on D_1, it is on the O_1 side of I_1^*.

   This is the geometric form of the properties announced above.

   The analogous properties with respect to individual 2 can be shown in a similar way.

c Equity, Efficiency, Equality

α *The General Case*
The essence of the above results is very simple:

If someone is "jealous," she prefers equality.
  With all the refinements, these properties are written:

$$x_1 \underset{1}{\succ} g \;\Rightarrow\; x_1 \underset{1}{\succ} x_2 \qquad x_2 \underset{2}{\succ} g \;\Rightarrow\; x_2 \underset{2}{\succ} x_1$$

$$x_1 \underset{1}{\succsim} g \;\Rightarrow\; x_1 \underset{1}{\succsim} x_2 \qquad x_2 \underset{2}{\succsim} g \;\Rightarrow\; x_2 \underset{2}{\succsim} x_1$$

$$x_2 \underset{1}{\succ} x_1 \;\Rightarrow\; g \underset{1}{\succ} x_1 \qquad x_1 \underset{2}{\succ} x_2 \;\Rightarrow\; g \underset{2}{\succ} x_2$$

$$x_2 \underset{1}{\succsim} x_1 \;\Rightarrow\; g \underset{1}{\succsim} x_1 \qquad x_1 \underset{2}{\succsim} x_2 \;\Rightarrow\; g \underset{2}{\succsim} x_2$$

and, with preferences having strict satiation at equality and
$x_1 \neq x_2 \neq g$,

$$x_1 \underset{1}{\succsim} g \;\Rightarrow\; x_1 \underset{1}{\succ} x_2 \qquad x_2 \underset{2}{\succsim} g \;\Rightarrow\; x_2 \underset{2}{\succ} x_1$$

$$x_2 \underset{1}{\succsim} x_1 \;\Rightarrow\; g \underset{1}{\succ} x_1 \qquad x_1 \underset{2}{\succsim} x_2 \;\Rightarrow\; g \underset{2}{\succ} x_2$$

The first two lines of this table give theorem 1.
  Geometrically, the locus Γ of the points representing distributions preferred to or equivalent to equality for both persons at the same time, is that portion of the space included between I_1^* and I_2^*, border included, and situated on the O_2 side of I_1^* and on the O_1 side of I_2^* (figure 16). Γ is, thus, according to the results obtained, on the O_2 side of D_1 and on the O_1 side of D_2. Consequently, Γ is contained in Q: $\Gamma \subseteq Q$. In other words, *the distributions unanimously preferred or equivalent to equality are equitable.*

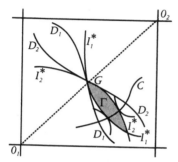

Figure 16

Moreover, there are points of Q that are not in Γ unless D_1 coincides with I_1^* and D_2 with I_2^*. This last condition would require that I_1^*, I_2^*, D_1, and D_2 are hyperplanes, because that is the only structure that permits the conjunction of satiation and of symmetry with respect to G for D_1 and D_2. In particular, the condition cannot be realized when the preferences of one of the individuals have strict satiation at equality. Thus, in general, and always in this last case, $\Gamma \subset Q$.

Denote as C the locus of points representing efficient distributions. At any point of C, a hypersurface I_1 and a hypersurface I_2 are tangent. C is in general a curve, *the contract curve*. It is always a curve if there is strict satiation of preferences for both individuals.

Since Γ is the locus of points that represent distributions that both individuals prefer or consider equivalent to a certain distribution, G, there exist some (at least one) points of Γ that represent efficient distributions. In other words, C and Γ have some (at least one) common points:

$$C \cap \Gamma \neq \varnothing.$$

And since Γ is in Q, these points are in Q. Consequently, C and Q have some (at least one) points in common:

$$C \cap Q \neq \varnothing.$$

Thus, *there are distributions that are both equitable and efficient.*

β The Case in Which Equality is Efficient

The case in which C and Γ have a single common point is the one in which I_1^* and I_2^* are tangent in a single point. Since these hypersurfaces pass through G, that is the point. Figure 17 shows this case for $m = 2$. Γ is reduced to G, and C passes through G. D_1 and D_2, tangent to I_1^* and I_2^* at G, also are tangent to cne another there. But, their symmetry with respect to G implies that they cross, in general, at G. For $n = 2$, the two curves D_1 and D_2 are osculatory at G. There is no distribution preferred or equivalent to equality for both persons, other than equality itself. But there are equitable distributions other than equality, since any point situated in a portion of space delimited by D_1 and D_2 and containing neither O_1 nor O_2, border included, either represents an equitable distribution, or is symmetric (with respect to G) to a point that represents an equitable distribution; and any point belonging

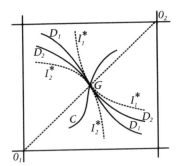

Figure 17

both to D_1 and D_2 represents an equitable distribution. However, since C crosses I_1^* and I_2^* at G, it also crosses D_1 and D_2 at G, and there is no distribution other than equality that is both efficient and equitable: *equality is the only distribution that is both efficient and equitable.*

It is possible, with nonstrict satiations, that I_1^* and I_2^* are tangent along the length of a linear element not reduced to a point. Because of satiation this element is a convex set and thus also a connected one, it contains all the points common to I_1^* and I_2^* and in particular it contains G. The points of this element represent distributions equivalent to equality for both individuals. These also are points of C, which no longer is reduced to a line. But there is no distribution preferred to equality by both persons, nor even preferred by one and equivalent for the other.

γ *Identical Preferences*

All these cases of tangency of I_1^* and I_2^* are fortuitous, with the exception of that one situation in which the two individuals have identical preferences (cf. part I, section C-1). In that situation I_1^* and I_2^* are each symmetric to the other with respect to their common point G from which it results that they are tangent at G. Moreover, the networks of indifference hypersurfaces I_1 and I_2 are each symmetric to the other with respect to G: any I_1' symmetric to an I_1 is an I_2 and any I_2' symmetric to an I_2 is an I_1. There results from this that the two hypersurfaces of the indifferent divisions D_1 and D_2 coincide (figure 18). The locus of points representing equitable distributions Q also reduces to the same hypersurface. The locus Γ of points representing distributions preferred or equivalent to equality for both individuals reduces to the point G itself if there is strict satiation there. If satiation is not strict at equality, all the

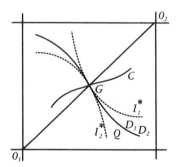

Figure 18

points of a connected linear element, containing G, symmetric with respect to G, situated in I_1^*, I_2^*, D_1, D_2, Q, and C, represent distributions equivalent to equality for both individuals, and no distribution is unanimously preferred to equality or even preferred by one and equivalent for the other: then, this linear element is Γ. Of course, C is symmetric with respect to G.

These results permit us easily to show theorems 6 and 7 in the case considered here of $n = 2$, and to enrich them with the cases of the situations in which satiation at equality is not necessarily strict. Theorem 6 is obvious. The corollary of theorem 7 results from the preceding constructions: with strict satiation at equality, G is the only point common to C and Q; if this condition is not satisfied, the intersection of C and Q is the linear element Γ that has been described above, and all its points represent distributions that are both equitable and efficient, and that also are equivalent to equality for each person. Theorem 7 is proven directly by construction of the hypersurface which is, simultaneously, D_1, D_2, and Q. Indeed, any equitable distribution is represented by a point of Q, which is therefore on an I_1 and an I_2 which are symmetric with respect to G. If these I_1 and I_2 are not I_1^* and I_2^*, they are respectively on the O_1 side of I_1^* and on the O_2 side of I_2^*, from which it results that each of the two individuals finds the distribution inferior to equality. If they are I_1^* and I_2^*, then if satiation is strict at equality, this point[4] is G and the distribution considered is equality; and if satiation is not

---

4. *Translator's note*: Representing any equitable distribution.

strict at equality, this point belongs to Γ as defined above, and the distribution that it represents therefore is equivalent to equality for each individual. Thus, the following results hold:

- With strict satiation at equality: *equality is unanimously preferred to all other equitable distributions.*

- In general: *equality is unanimously preferred or equivalent to all equitable distributions.*

- With strict satiation at equality: *equality is the only equitable and efficient distribution.*

- In general: *any equitable and efficient distribution is equivalent to equality for both individuals, and conversely.*

δ *Indivisibilities*
A result concerning the case in which there are indivisible goods will be shown in the next section: equity entails efficiency when there is a single divisible good.

2 Processes

We now examine the properties of certain distribution *processes* between two persons. We will study two of them: *divide and choose* and *bilateral exchange*. This analysis can be made thanks to the preceding analytical apparatus, which will be completed or specified as necessary.

a Divide and Choose

α *The Problem*

One has quantities of an unspecified number of goods. One
of two individuals divides this whole X of resources into
two lots. The other person *chooses* the lots she prefers,
thereby, *ipso facto*, leaving the other lot to the first person.
What is the resulting distribution? What are the properties
of this distribution from the point of view of equity, of
efficiency, of preference to equality, and of the advantage
in having one of the two roles rather than the other?

In order to make his decision, the divider anticipates the
choice of the chooser facing the two lots. What the divider
knows of the preferences of the chooser therefore is
important. We will consider several situations from this
point of view. The most important situation will be the
central case in which the divider has perfect knowledge of
all she needs to know of the preferences of the chooser.
Next we will consider the case in which the divider does
not know the preferences of the chooser and exercises
extreme prudence, which leads her to consider the worst
possible choice by the chooser: this is what is called
"minimax" behavior ("to minimize the maximum risk").
Finally we will consider the case in which the chooser can
make the divider believe that her preferences have a certain
structure. It is quite evident that in the first two cases the
chooser's state of knowledge of the preferences of the
divider does not matter; but we will show that the same is
true in the third case as well.

The properties of information should always be understood as applying "for the useful elements, and in the useful

domains." In order to avoid analytical refinements that would distract us from the essential characteristics of the process, strict satiation will be assumed. The divider will be denoted as individual 1 and the chooser as individual 2.

A division performed by individual 1 is represented, in the space previously considered, by a pair of points M and M' that are symmetric with respect to G. This division by individual 1 being made, individual 2, in choosing one of the lots, assigns the lots to individuals 1 and 2 respectively, that is, she chooses between the two distributions represented by M and M'. Individual 2 is indifferent between the two distributions if M and M' are on D_2. Otherwise, she prefers one to the other.

If M and M' are not on D_2, they are on opposite sides of this hypersurface because it is symmetric with respect to G. If M is on the O_1 side of D_2, individual 2 prefers her lot to that of individual 1 in this distribution, that is, she prefers M to M'. On the other hand, if M is on the O_2 side of D_2, individual 2 prefers the lot of individual 1 to her own lot in this distribution, that is, she prefers M' to M, and M' is on the O_1 side of D_2.

Consequently, individual 2 always chooses a point located on the O_1 side of D_2, the border D_2 included. And individual 1 can impose as the final result any point located on the O_1 side of D_2 by choosing the corresponding division. Thus, the constraint that this process imposes on individual 1's choice of distribution is that the M that corresponds to it must be in this domain. Hence, individual 1 tries to choose the division that corresponds to the point in this domain that is best for her. Therefore, her knowledge of D_2 comes into play, and, consequently, so does her knowledge of the preferences of individual 2.

β Perfect Knowledge

If individual 1 has perfect knowledge of everything she needs to know, she will choose the division corresponding to a point K at which the hypersurface of indifference I_1 of individual 1 passing through K is tangent to D_2 (figure 19). However, if K is precisely on D_2, we do not know whether individual 2 will choose K or the point symmetric to K with respect to G, since she is indifferent between them. To avoid this uncertainty, individual 1 can choose a point infinitely close to K and located on the O_1 side of D_2. But one can assimilate this point with K because infinitely small distances and quantities do not have economic significance (in reality, the distance between the point chosen and K must just exceed the "threshold of discernment" of individual 2, something that the representation of preferences does not take into account).

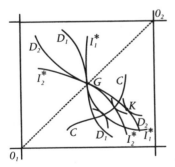

Figure 19

Individual 1 could have chosen equality, G. She therefore finds K at least as good as G. Thus, K is on the O_2 side of I_1^* (or may be on I_1^*). It follows from a preceding result that K is on the O_2 side of D_1 (or possibly on D_1). Since it is also on D_2 (or very near D_2 on the O_1 side), it is equitable: the process, therefore, is *equitable*.

It is possible that K is at G. This happens if, and only if, I_1^*, I_2^*, D_1, and D_2, are tangent at this point. C then passes through G. In this case, K is in Γ and is efficient. But in the other cases, K is neither in Γ nor on C, and the (divide and choose) process is not unanimously preferred or indifferent to equality, nor is it efficient.

This is so because K is on D_2 and D_2 is on the O_2 side of I_2^* except for G which belongs to both hypersurfaces. Consequently, if K is not at G it is on the O_2 side of I_2^* and individual 2 prefers G to K.

In this case, again, since I_1^* and I_2^* cross at G, there are points unanimously preferred to G (interior points of Γ). These points are on the O_1 side of I_2^* and thus of D_2. Individual 1 therefore prefers K to these points. But she prefers these points to G. She therefore prefers K to G.

Consequently, when the result is not equality, *the person who divides prefers this process to equality, and the person who chooses prefers equality to this process.* It results that *each person would be better off to be the one who divides rather than the one who chooses.*

Furthermore, when K is not at G, the hypersurface I_2 that passes through the point K of D_2 is not tangent there to D_2 (as is shown in the heuristic construction of D_2); whereas the hypersurface I_1 that passes through K is tangent there to D_2. Thus, the hypersurfaces I_1 and I_2 that pass through K are not tangent to one another there. Consequently, K is not on C: *the process is not efficient.*

These remarks prove theorem 2.

These results give a good evaluation of the "divide and choose" process in this case. It guarantees equity. But, it does so "in extremis" in a sense because K is on the D_2 border of Q. And this process also almost guarantees inefficiency. Moreover, because one of the two roles is better than the other for each person, there is from the beginning a certain injustice. Finally, because divide and choose is better than equality for one of the two individuals but inferior for the other, it is impossible to have this "rule of the game" unanimously accepted a priori by using equality as the "threat situation." But if the chooser can use this threat during the game, the divider chooses the division that corresponds to her best allocation on I_2^* (figure 19; in fact she chooses a division very close to it but preferred by the chooser), with a result that is equitable, practically efficient, unanimously preferred to equality, better for the chooser and worse for the divider than without the threat, but still such that each player prefers to be divider than chooser. This initial injustice (and, perhaps, this impossibility in agreeing to play the game) can be removed by selecting the two roles (divider and chooser) by lot with equal chances.

All possible defects and asymmetries disappear only in the "trivial" case in which the process yields equality, that is, in which I_1^* is tangent to D_2 at G and K is at G.[5] The process then is efficient and gives the same lot to both—whatever therefore their respective roles. But this situation is not entirely fortuitous only in the case in which the preferences of the two protagonists are identical. Then, D_1 and D_2 being coincident, I_1^* is entirely on the O_2 side of D_2, except for the point G that they have in common: K, therefore, necessarily is G.

γ *The Divider Does Not Know the Chooser's Preferences*
If individual 1 does not know D_2, then the process cannot function as described. This happens if individual 1 does not know the preferences of individual 2. What happens in this case? In choosing the equal division, the divider can impose equality with certainty. Thus, she will abstain from choosing a division from which she is sure the resulting distribution will be less desirable to her than equality. This happens in two types of cases (figure 20). The first assumes that the divider at least knows the nonsatiety property of the preferences of the chooser. The second does not assume even that.

If one of the lots contains at most half the quantity of each good and for at least one good it contains less than half the quantity of that good, so that the other lot contains at least half the quantity of each good and more than half the quantity of at least one good, then the divider is certain that the chooser will choose the second lot and will leave

---

5. The fact that G is efficient and I_1^* tangent to D_2 at G does not necessarily imply that K is at G.

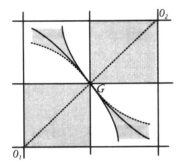

Figure 20

the divider the first lot, that is, if the divider knows that the chooser is satiated in none of these goods. But, the first lot is less desirable to the divider than is equality, which attributes to her half the quantity of each good. Therefore, the points M or M' thus "dominated" by G or "dominating" G are excluded.

On the other hand, neither will the divider select a division in which he finds both lots inferior to equality. This happens when points M and M' (symmetric with respect to G) are both on the O_1 side of I_1^*. But, if one of these points is on the O_1 side of I_1^*, the other is on the O_2 side of the hypersurface $I_1^{*\prime}$ symmetric to I_1^* with respect to G. Consequently, the distributions thereby excluded are those for which the representative points are in the zone that is delimited by I_1^* and $I_1^{*\prime}$, and where neither O_1 nor O_2 is located, the zone between I_1^* and $I_1^{*\prime}$. This zone is symmetric with respect to point G. It contains the hypersurface D_1 because D_1 is on the O_1 side of I_1^* and is symmetric with respect to G: In the symmetry that transforms I_1^* into $I_1^{*\prime}$, D_1 is transformed into a hypersurface located on the O_2 side of $I_1^{*\prime}$ and which is itself.

Outside this zone and its border, one of the points M or M' is on the O_2 side of I_1^*. The divider prefers one of the two lots to equality, and prefers equality to the other lot. Satiation of preferences of individual 1 prevents M and M' from both being on the O_2 side of I_1^*, or even from both being on I_1^* and not at G: the divider cannot create two lots, both of which she prefers to equality, and neither can she create unequal lots such that she does not prefer equality to each of them. If M or M' is on I_1^* and not at G, then for the divider it is equivalent to equality, and the other point is inferior to it and to equality; in this case, the divider prefers to create equal lots if there is some chance that the chooser may attribute the inferior lot to her. Thus, with this qualification, *the divider always creates two lots of which she prefers one to equality, and equality to the other; unless she creates two equal lots.* In the first case she takes the risk of receiving a lot that she judges less desirable than equality in order to attempt to obtain one that she prefers to equality. In the second case she does not take this risk.

Equal division is what is chosen by an extremely prudent divider, who acts as if "the worst is always certain" and thus has what game theory calls a minimax attitude (minimize the maximum risk)—she acts so that the worst distribution which may happen is the best she can secure, and, therefore, she takes into account only that choice of the chooser that is worse for the divider. Indeed, we have seen that either the two lots are inferior to equality for the divider, or the worse of the two is inferior to equality, or the choice is equality. Thus, except for equality the worse lot for the divider is inferior to equality for her. A divider having the indicated (minimax) attitude therefore chooses equality.

This property also obtains directly. Of the two points M and M' which are symmetric with respect to G and represent a division, one is on the O_1 side of D_1, and that point represents a distribution that for individual 1 is worse than its permutation; at the limit both points are on D_1 and are equivalent for the individual. Individual 1 is concerned only about this worse state. Of the points that are on the O_1 side of D_1, or are on D_1, G is the best (for her) that she can realize without risk (by dividing equally).

This result can be obtained in yet another interesting way. It consists in noting that this behavior of the divider amounts to her acting as if the chooser's preferences were the same as hers. In this case, indeed, the chooser, by choosing the better of the two lots, always will leave the worse lot to the divider. But, if the preferences of the two are identical, the situation is that in which the K of the preceding section is at G.

In this case, the result of the "divide and choose" process, equality, is equitable. Moreover, it does not depend on the roles of the parties: the result is the same whoever divides or chooses. This reinforces the quality of justice of this process. But the result, in general, is not efficient. The exception is again the case when equality is efficient.

Consequently, in these two extreme cases of the divider's knowledge of the preferences of the chooser (perfect knowledge and ignorance with a minimax attitude), the process of divide and choose is *equitable and inefficient*, except that the process is efficient when it yields equality and that state of equality is efficient. Moreover, it is never preferable to be the one who chooses rather than the one who divides. Equality is never inferior to divide and choose for the chooser and never superior for the divider.

The results obtained in these two cases (in particular theorem 2) show that the divider and the chooser have divergent interests with respect to information: the divider prefers to have such knowledge while the chooser is better off if the divider is ignorant. But in this process the question is only knowledge of the chooser's preferences and not knowledge of the divider's preferences. The chooser, therefore, has an interest in hiding her preferences from the divider.

δ *Perfect Deception*

The chooser may even be able to do better by deceiving the divider into believing that the chooser's preferences are different from what they really are. What is the resulting state? What are its properties?

We will assume that one has the constraints $x_i^j \geq 0$ for all i, j and that the only other constraints are those of distribution. The ideal for the chooser would be to make the divider believe that she has an aversion to all the commodities. The divider would then create two lots, one containing everything and the other containing nothing.

She would do this counting on obtaining the first lot. But the chooser would take it herself. The chooser would have everything, and the divider would have nothing. But in general the divider knows that the chooser has no reason to reject the commodities, and even that the chooser is not indifferent among all possible distributions. Then the best that the chooser can do is to feign indifference as to all the commodities except one. This commodity will be chosen in the following manner. Call L_i a lot composed of half the total quantity of commodity i and of all the quantities of all the other commodities, that is,

$$L_i = x^1, x^2, ..., x^{i-1}, \frac{x^i}{2}, x^{i+1}, ..., x^m.$$

The only commodity for which the chooser does not feign indifference is the one such that the L_i that corresponds to it is preferred by the chooser to all the others. If several L_i are preferred or indifferent to all the others, this commodity is any one of these i. Let us relabel this commodity i as commodity 1 (figure 21). We thus have

$$L_1 \underset{\sim}{\succ} L_i \qquad \text{for all } i.$$

If the divider knows that the chooser is not indifferent to the other goods, the chooser will feign *nearly* total indifference towards them.

Then, the divider creates two lots. One contains only $x^1/2$. The other contains $x^1/2$ plus all of each of the other commodities. More precisely, these lots are

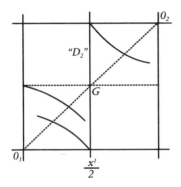

Figure 21

$$\lambda = \frac{x^1}{2} + \varepsilon, \ 0, \ 0, \ ..., \ 0$$

and

$$\mu = \frac{x^1}{2} - \varepsilon, \ x^2, \ x^3, \ ..., \ x^m,$$

ε being a very small quantity of good 1 designed to ascertain, in the mind of the divider, that the chooser will prefer λ to μ. But, given these lots, the chooser instead takes μ and leaves λ to the divider, thus approximately realizing the distribution

$$x_1 = \frac{x^1}{2}, \ 0, \ 0, \ ..., \ 0$$

$$x_2 = \frac{x^1}{2}, \ x^2, \ x^3, \ ..., \ x^m.$$

The result is *better than equality for the chooser and worse than equality for the divider. It is therefore better to have the role of the chooser than that of the divider. The divider prefers the chooser's lot to her own. The process therefore is inequitable.* By these properties, this case is in *opposition* to the one in which the divider has perfect knowledge of the preferences of the chooser. On the other hand, the *chooser prefers her lot to that of the divider,* and the process is in general *inefficient,* as in the case of perfect knowledge. Note that to realize this distribution *the chooser need not know anything about the preferences of the divider* (except nonsatiety). The process amounts to the chooser making the divider believe that the chooser's hypersurface of equivalent divisions D_2 is the hyperplane of the equation $x_1^1 = x_2^1 = x^1/2$ (or a hypersurface very close to it).

ε *Indivisibilities*
In all this analysis of the problems of distribution, we have assumed that the quantities to be distributed are perfectly divisible. But it is easy to see that the existence of indivisibilities can substantially change the problem. For example, equal distribution, which played an important role in all the reasoning, in general no longer exists. Therefore, this section examines a case of indivisibility—in fact, the simplest case and thus the first one that must be considered—: the case in which there is a single indivisible element, and only one divisible "commodity," to be divided

between two persons. The results and the properties of the "divide and choose" process are analyzed in this context.

Let us denote the indivisible element as a, the total quantity of the unidimensional divisible element as X, and the quantity of this element that is associated with a in order to form a lot as x. The other lot consists of the remaining quantity $X - x$ of this element. This model can represent several types of problems. In one, X is a quantity of a divisible good that is desired by both persons, they also desire a, and one has $X > 0$, $x \geq 0$, $X - x \geq 0$. Of course, these quantities, like a, also can be of services to be received. But a can, more generally, be any set of goods, rights, obligations, etc., simple or complex. And, these persons may or may not desire it, and they may have on this point similar or opposite desires. Similarly, the divisible quantities can represent a liability of a service or of a good that the holder must provide. If this is the case, we measure them negatively, that is, X, x, or $X - x$ are negative, so the persons prefer the number measuring what they have of it to be larger. We then may have the sign constraints: $X < 0$, $x \leq 0$, $X - x \leq 0$. But these constraints may not exist so that some of these numbers can be positive and others negative. One may, for example, have $X = 0$ if the divisible element is a quantity of a service provided by one person to the other. However, it will always be assumed that the lots are possible no matter who receives them.

Denoting the two persons as individuals 1 and 2, the lot constituted by a and by the quantity x as (a, x), and the other lot as $X - x$, x_1 and x_2 are defined by

$$(a, x_1) \underset{1}{\tilde{}} X - x_1,$$

and

$$(a, x_2) \underset{2}{\tilde{}} X - x_2.$$

As previously, only the preference orderings matter. Given the definition of the divisible quantities, and assuming that the individuals are not satiated for them in the useful domain, it follows that the levels x_1 and x_2 are all that matter with respect to the individuals' preferences. The "divide and choose" process will be considered in two states of the divider's knowledge of the chooser's preferences and of the divider's behavior: perfect knowledge, and ignorance with a minimax behavior. The symbol ε will denote a very small quantity of the divisible commodity capable of influencing the decision of the chooser in the choices in which it will intervene. The divider's act consists of choosing x.

The following questions are posed. In each case of knowledge and type of behavior, is the process equitable? Is it efficient? Is it better to divide than to choose, or vice versa, and by how much as measured in quantity of the divisible "commodity?" How do these results depend on whether the divider or the chooser has the larger x_1 or x_2?

Denote the divider as individual 1 and the chooser as individual 2.

First, consider the case of perfect knowledge, that is, individual 1 knows x_2.

Consider, to begin with, the case in which $x_2 > x_1$. If $x > x_2$, the chooser chooses (a, x) and leaves $X - x$ to the divider. But, since also $x > x_1$, $X - x < X - x_1$. However, the divider always can ensure for herself $X - x_1$ or its equivalent for her (a, x_1), by making $x = x_1$. Consequently, the divider selects an $x \le x_2$, and the chooser chooses $X - x$ and leaves (a, x) to the divider. The best of these x's for the divider is x_2, or rather $x_2 - \varepsilon$ in order to be sure that the chooser chooses $X - x_2 + \varepsilon$, leaving $(a, x_2 - \varepsilon)$ to the divider.

If $x_2 < x_1$, it can be shown in a similar fashion that $x = x_2 + \varepsilon$, and the result is that the chooser has $(a, x_2 + \varepsilon)$ while the divider has $X - x_2 - \varepsilon$.

Next, consider the case in which the divider does not know x_2 and she wants to "minimize the maximum risk." One of the two lots is $X - x$, and the other is (a, x). If $x > x_1$, one of the two lots is $X - x$ which is smaller than $X - x_1$ and therefore is less desirable to individual 1 than $X - x_1$. If $x < x_1$, one of the two lots is (a, x) which is less desirable for individual 1 than (a, x_1). Consequently, the divider makes $x = x_1$. The chooser chooses (a, x_1) if $x_2 < x_1$ and chooses $X - x_1$ if $x_2 > x_1$. She leaves to the divider $X - x_1$ or (a, x_1), respectively, which are indifferent to the divider.

In all these cases, the process is *equitable*. Indeed, the chooser never prefers the divider's lot to her own, or she would have chosen it. In the "ignorance and minimax" case the divider is indifferent between the lots. In the case of perfect knowledge, if $x_2 > x_1$, we have

$$(a, x_2) \underset{1}{\succ} (a, x_1) \underset{1}{\sim} X - x_1 \underset{1}{\succ} X - x_2,$$

and if $x_2 < x_1$, we have

$$X - x_2 \underset{1}{\succ} X - x_1 \underset{1}{\widetilde{}} (a, x_1) \underset{1}{\succ} (a, x_2).$$

Thus, the divider prefers her own lot to that of the chooser. This completes the proof of the property.

The results of the process also prove the following properties:

- *Knowledge is better than "ignorance and minimax" for the divider, but worse for the chooser.*

- *With perfect knowledge, it is better to divide than to choose.*

- *With "ignorance and minimax," it is better to choose than to divide.*

In all these cases, the gain or loss is equal to the quantity $|x_1 - x_2|$ of the divisible commodity if one has only that commodity (ignoring ε).

Finally, in all cases the process is *efficient*. Surprisingly, this property requires the most extended proof. To prove the property, we must show that for each distribution other than the one realized, one of the two individuals finds it inferior to the realized distribution. If in the two distributions being compared, the same person has the item a, that is, the only difference between the two distributions is the level of x, this property is obvious. It is sufficient, therefore, to consider the cases in which the item a belongs to one individual in one distribution, but to the other individual in the other distribution, that is, there is a *change in attribution* of the item *a*. There are four possible situations to consider: perfect knowledge or "ignorance and minimax," and in each case $x_1 > x_2$ or $x_2 > x_1$. Indeed, if $x_1 = x_2$, then this is the level of x realized in all cases, both individuals are indifferent to the attribution, and, therefore, in order to compare the realized state with others, one can begin by changing the attribution and then compare the x and $X - x$: there always is one of the two individuals who loses from the change. Let ξ be the level of x in the distribution considered that is not implemented by the process. The ε can be ignored.

1) *Perfect Knowledge*
The x achieved is x_2, and $(a, x_2) \underset{2}{\sim} X - x_2$.

α) $x_1 < x_2$.

In the realized state, individual 1 has (a, x_2) and individual 2 has $X - x_2$. In the unrealized state, a is attributed to individual 2. If $\xi < x_2$, then individual 2 is worse off in the unrealized state. If $\xi > x_2$ (and thus $\xi > x_1$), then, for individual 1,

$$X - \xi \underset{1}{\prec} X - x_1 \underset{1}{\sim} (a, x_1) \underset{1}{\prec} (a, x_2),$$

and, therefore, individual 1 is worse off in the unrealized states.

β) $x_1 > x_2$.

In the realized state, individual 1 has $X - x_2$ and individual 2 has (a, x_2). In the unrealized state, a is attributed to individual 1 and individual 2 has $X - \xi$. If $\xi > x_2$, individual 2 is worse off in the unrealized state. If $\xi < x_2$ (and, therefore, $\xi < x_1$), then, for individual 1,

$$(a, \xi) \underset{1}{\prec} (a, x_1) \underset{1}{\sim} X - x_1 \underset{1}{\prec} X - x_2,$$

and, therefore, individual 1 is worse off in the unrealized state.

2) *Minimax*
The x realized is x_1, and $(a, x_1) \underset{1}{\sim} X - x_1$.

α) $x_1 < x_2$.

In the realized state, individual 2 chooses $X - x_1$ and leaves (a, x_1) to individual 1. Thus, for the unrealized state, if $\xi > x_1$, then $X - \xi < X - x_1$, and individual 1 is worse off. If $\xi < x_1$ (and, therefore, $\xi < x_2$),

$$(a, \xi) \underset{2}{\prec} (a, x_2) \underset{2}{\sim} X - x_2 \underset{2}{\prec} X - x_1,$$

and, therefore, individual 2 is worse off.

β) $x_1 > x_2$.

In the realized state, individual 2 chooses (a, x_1) and leaves $X - x_1$ to individual 1. Thus, for the unrealized state, if $\xi < x_1$, then $(a, \xi) \underset{1}{\prec} (a, x_1)$ and individual 1 is worse off. If $\xi > x_1$ (and, therefore, $\xi > x_2$),

$$X - \xi \underset{2}{\prec} X - x_2 \underset{2}{\sim} (a, x_2) \underset{2}{\prec} (a, x_1)$$

and, therefore, individual 2 is worse off.

Finally, let us compare the properties of the case involving indivisibility with those of the case involving complete divisibility (in the general case with regard to the structure of preferences and for the same characteristics of information and behavior). Many of the points are common:

- *Equity.*

- *Advantage of knowledge for the divider.*

- *Advantage of dividing rather than choosing in the case of perfect knowledge.*

But there also are some important differences:

- *In the case of an ignorant divider with a minimax attitude, then, given divisibility, it does not matter whether one divides or chooses, whereas, given indivisibility, it is better to choose than to divide.*

- *The process is inefficient with divisibility and efficient with indivisibility.*

Note that the proof of efficiency with indivisibility shows that efficiency results only from equity. However, if there were several divisible commodities and one or

several indivisible commodities, the outcome of the process
would generally be inefficient.

b Bilateral Exchange

Since exchange is the special case of distribution in which
$X = g = 0$ and in which the x_i^j can be of any sign, all of the
preceding analysis of distribution between two persons
applies to bilateral exchange. The case $m = 2$ is of particular interest with respect to problems of exchange because it
is more common for two persons to exchange two commodities than for them to engage in a complex transaction
involving more than two commodities. This is in particular
the case for purchases and sales of monetary exchanges, in
which one of the two commodities is money. A bilateral
exchange is equitable if each participant prefers that
exchange to one in which she would give up that which she
receives and would receive that which she gives up.

The exchange can be represented in the m-dimensional
Euclidean space with the axes measuring the quantities
exchanged. Measure a quantity received by individual 1
and given up by individual 2 positively and measure a
quantity given up by individual 1 and received by individual 2 negatively. Figure 22 shows the problem in the case
of two commodities ($m = 2$). The origin O is the state
without exchange. I_1 and I_2 denote the indifference hypersurfaces of individuals 1 and 2, respectively, and I_1^* and I_2^*
are the I_1 and I_2 that pass through O. A bilateral exchange
represented by a point M is equitable if each person prefers
this state to the one that is represented by the point M'

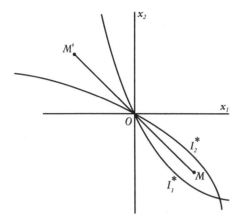

Figure 22

symmetric to M with respect to O or is indifferent between them.

Free exchange, in which each participant has the right to choose O, necessarily yields a state that is preferred (or equivalent) by both to O. Let M be the point representing the realized exchange, and M' the point that is symmetric to M with respect to O. Writing the preferences between these states, and taking account of the forms of the hypersurfaces I_1^* and I_2^* due to satiation of preferences, we have

$$M \underset{1}{\succsim} O \underset{1}{\succsim} M'$$

and

$$M \underset{2}{\succsim} O \underset{2}{\succsim} M'$$

(if M and M' are both on O, they are equivalent for the two persons). It follows from this that *free bilateral exchange is equitable* (theorem 3). In fact, this result was implicit in theorem 1 since the states realizable by free exchange are the ones that are unanimously preferred or indifferent to the state without exchange which corresponds here to equality.

Call a series of free exchanges between two persons a *sequential free exchange*. The result of a sequential free exchange is judged by reference to the initial state. For each free exchange, the resulting state is unanimously preferred or equivalent to the state of departure. But that state of departure is the state resulting from the preceding free exchange or it is the initial state. It follows from this that the final resulting state of a sequential free exchange is unanimously preferred or equivalent to the initial state. Consequently, *sequential bilateral free exchange is equitable*.

However, if the starting state of a free exchange and the origin of the measures of quantities are not in this kind of relation (for instance the same state), the outcome of a free exchange of course can be inequitable, and it can be so even if the starting state is equitable (see part III, section A.4, figure 25), although if this state is in addition efficient no mutually profitable and free exchange can start from it.

B Any Number of Persons

1 Compatibility of Equity, Efficiency, and Unanimous Preference to Equality

Using the previous general remark that individuals' choices in identical domains entail equity, the preceding description of distributions (of given divisible quantities) that have the three properties of equity, efficiency, and unanimous preference or equivalence to equality, is straightforwardly specified, and extended to any number of persons, by the consideration of perfect market equilibrium with equal incomes, which can result from an equal initial distribution. Indeed, it is known that for any initial allocation of resources, given the assumed satiation, there exists a perfect market equilibrium which is an allocation of goods having the following properties. The total quantities of goods are the same as in the initial allocation (that is, the quantity supplied and the quantity demanded of each good is equal). It is an efficient state. There is a system of prices, with which the values of the allocations are measured. Each person prefers her market allocation to any other not having a higher value, or is indifferent between the two. The values of the initial allocations and of the market allocations of each person are equal. In other words, any allocation preferred by one person to her market allocation has a value higher than that of her initial and market allocations. These characteristics show, among other things, that each person prefers her market allocation to her initial allocation, or is indifferent between them. If, furthermore, the values of the person's initial allocations happen to be equal, from which there results that their market allocations also are of equal value, each person prefers her market allocation to that of each other person, or is indifferent between them. That is, this market allocation is an equitable state. Therefore, the choice of the equal distribution as the initial allocation of a perfect market leads to a state that has the three properties of efficiency, equity,[6] and unanimous preference or equivalence to equality. If the commodities considered result from production and transformation whose efficiency becomes relevant also (and are performed with the classical convex possibility sets), the same result is obtained by a perfect market equilibrium with an equal sharing of the ownership of initial resources and of firms (equal sharing of profits).

This equilibrium can be represented geometrically in representing the individuals' allocations in the same coordinate system with origin O (figure 23 for the case of two commodities). These individuals' "budget hyperplanes" coincide because they all pass through point g and have the same normal (which is the direction of the price vector). Each person's equilibrium allocation is represented by a point at which one of this person's indifference hypersurfaces is tangent to the budget hyperplane. All the other points of the budget hyperplane are on the side of this indifference hypersurface that represents allocations inferior to the point of tangency or are on this indifference hypersurface. This is, in particular, the case of the equal distribution g and of the equilibrium allocations of the other persons.

---

6. See the historical introduction.

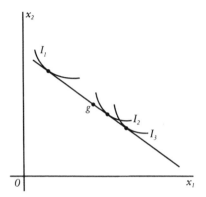

Figure 23

In other words, if $\xi = \{x_1, ..., x_n\}$ is the perfect market equilibrium allocation obtained from the equal distribution, and p is the price vector (which multiplies scalarly with the x_i), we have

$$\Sigma x_i = X,$$

$$px_i = pg \qquad \text{for all } i,$$

thus

$$x_i \underset{i}{\succeq} g \qquad \text{for all } i,$$

$$x_i \underset{i}{\succeq} x_{i'} \qquad \text{for all pairs } i \text{ and } i',$$

and ξ is efficient. Therefore *there exists at least one distribution that is equitable, efficient, and unanimously preferred or equivalent to equality.*

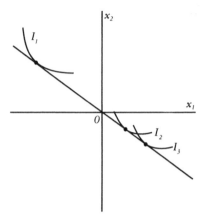

Figure 24

In particular, if we set $X = 0$, so that $g = 0$, we see that a perfect market, and, in particular, perfect competition, is not only efficient but also equitable with respect to exchanges (that is, theorem 4' and its corollaries) (figure 24).

Minimal equity amounts to equity for $n = 2$, but it is only implied by it for $n > 2$. The property, valid for $n = 2$, that unanimous preference to equality implies equity applies, for $n > 2$, not to equity but to minimal equity. Indeed, from satiation of individual i's preferences, $g \underset{i}{\succ} x_i$ if $x_j \underset{i}{\succ} x_i$ for all j (individual i's "general envy or jealousy"), and $g \underset{i}{\succsim} x_i$ if $x_j \underset{i}{\succsim} x_i$ for all j. Hence the lemma and theorem 5.

2 Identical Preferences

Theorems 6 and 7 have been proved for two persons. Let us prove them now for any number of persons.

a Properties of Satiation

Start from the following properties of convex preferences. x_i is a vector of commodities on which these preferences are displayed. There are n such vectors: $i = 1, ..., n$. The summations are over all the i. Preference and indifference are represented classically by $\succ, \sim, \succsim$. These preferences are always assumed to have satiation, and we will sometimes add that preferences with strict satiation at a designated point are considered (this structure exists in particular if the preferences are strict everywhere). The following properties hold.

Properties 1 and 2 concern the case in which all the x_i are equivalent.

1. If all the x_i are equivalent,

$$\frac{\sum x_i}{n} \succsim x_i.$$

2. If all the x_i are equivalent, if satiation is strict at $\frac{\sum x_i}{n}$, and if the x_i are not all identical,

$$\frac{\sum x_i}{n} \succ x_i.$$

Properties 3 and 4 are more general and include properties 1 and 2 as particular cases.

3. $\frac{\sum x_i}{n}$ is preferred or equivalent to the least desirable x_i.

4. If the x_i are not all identical and if satiation is strict at $\dfrac{\Sigma x_i}{n}$, then $\dfrac{\Sigma x_i}{n}$ is preferred to the least desirable x_i.

Finally, the particularly interesting property 5 holds.

5. If the x_i are not all equivalent, $\dfrac{\Sigma x_i}{n}$ is preferred to the least desirable x_i.

b Equality, Equity, Efficiency

Consider now a distribution problem with identical preferences. n persons i with the same preferences $\succ$, $\sim$, and $\succeq$ share $X = ng$, each having x_i. Since the preferences are identical, as we have seen above, a distribution is equitable if and only if all the x_i are equivalent for these preferences. Since it is a distribution problem, $\Sigma x_i = X$, and

$$\frac{\Sigma x_i}{n} = g.$$

Properties 1 and 2 therefore concern equitable distributions, and they are written

$$g \succeq x_i$$

and

$$g \succ x_i$$

for all i. Thus, *equality is unanimously preferred or equivalent to all equitable distributions; and if satiation is strict at equality, then equality is unanimously preferred to all other equitable distributions.*

Furthermore, if equality were not efficient, there would be a set of x_i such that $x_i \succsim g$ for all i, and $x_i \succ g$ for at least one i. But, if the x_i are not all equivalent, from property 5 g is preferred to the least desirable x_i. Thus, one does not have $x_i \succsim g$ for all i. And, if all the x_i are equivalent, from to property 1, $g \succsim x_i$ for all i, and, thus, there is no i for which $x_i \succ g$. In each case one of the two conditions is not satisfied, and therefore *equality is efficient.*

Finally, if satiation is strict at equality, no other equitable distribution can be efficient because everyone prefers equality to it (property 2). Thus, *equality is the only equitable and efficient distribution.*

III JUSTICE

A Justice and Equity

1 Fundamental Preference

Fundamentally, all individuals have the same needs, the same tastes and the same desires. This assertion undoubtedly demands an explanation. If two individuals have satisfaction preferences that appear to differ, there is a reason for it. There is something that makes them different from one another. Put this "something" formally in the *object of the preferences*, and thereby take the "something" out of the *parameters* that determine the structure of these preferences. The preferences of these two individuals, thus defined, are necessarily identical. The parameters thus transferred to the object of preferences of course may not be able to take the same values for different individuals (for example, age, sex, education received, most physical characteristics by which one person differs from another, and genetic stock). But this is now another problem that depends on the question of the domain of possible states, and no longer on the question of preferences.

The items that are so transferred from one class of variables to the other are the capacities to be satisfied or happy, to derive satisfaction or happiness, from each given situation, or the causes of these capacities (past experience, education, physiological traits, etc.). Along with the narrowly defined situation, they cause happiness or satisfaction which are thus interpersonally compared while remaining ordinal concepts. This comparison is required by eudemonistic social justice, and this eudemonistic conception of preferences is a classical—and the original—conception of "utility" that may represent these preferences. Such a comparison is actually possible in a certain domain which ex-

tends with more information. The behaviorist conception of
preferences as only a law of observed individual choices is
not our present topic, if only because many of the transferred parameters are not or cannot be objects of actual
choices. Yet this does not prevent people from actually
having and expressing preferences about these items: they
would prefer to be more sensitive to good things and less
to bad ones, to be satisfied with more easily available or
less expensive consumption alternatives, and to have
received the corresponding education. They think this
would make them happier (in particular). They indeed
consequently affect their own tastes and consumptive
capacities when they can, through education, information,
understanding, training, exercising awareness, trying to lose
habits or to become used to certain things, and so on.

For any society, the same operation can be performed:
that is, to put in the *object* of preferences anything that
would create differences in satisfaction among the various
members of the society. A preference thus obtained that is
identical for all members of this society is called a *funda-*
mental preference of these members. A fundamental
preference is a property that describes the tastes and needs
of the "representative individual" of this society in the
sense of the "common denominator" individual (rather than
of some "average individual"). But one can obtain identical
preferences in transferring a larger number of parameters
than is strictly necessary for this result (the extra parameters
are identical for all individuals). Then, when fewer parameters are transferred in the object of the preferences, the
fundamental preference contains more information about the
society. Thus, the preference that is particularly interesting

is the one obtained by passing to the object of the preferences the smallest possible set of parameters necessary to obtain identity of preferences (they constitute a "largest common denominator"). If this society is the set of all human beings, then what this concept fundamentally captures is "human nature."[1]

Fundamental preferences rank happiness or satisfaction derived from its causes of any possible kind. Since "happier" or "more satisfied" are likely to be transitive relations, fundamental preferences are assumed to have the structure of an ordering, with the possibility of indifferences. If this ordering is representable by an ordinal function, this is fundamental utility. A specification of this ordinal function orders levels of happiness or satisfaction both for each individual and across the individuals of this society.

Fundamental analysis is analysis using fundamental preferences. This part presents its basic concepts.

2 Definition of (eudemonistic) Justice

With fundamental preferences so defined for a society, eudemonistic or welfarist justice in this society can only mean that the individuals' overall situations are in the same fundamental indifference class (equal level of satisfaction). If the fundamental preference ordering can be represented by an ordinal utility function, this justice becomes *equality*

---

1. What is common to the other capacities of individuals also must be added.

of the utilities of the different persons. This property will henceforth be referred to as "justice," for short.

One question is naturally posed: what are the relations between equity as studied above and justice?

3 Fundamental Equity

Fundamental equity in a society is equity with fundamental preferences. When equity is not fundamental, we say that it is a *partial equity*.

Since fundamental preferences are by definition identical for all members of the society, according to a prior result there is fundamental equity if and only if the states of the individuals all belong to the same indifference class. Consequently, *fundamental equity is identical to justice.*

When a state is just, the situations of the members of society are generally not identical. In general, even, certain parameters cannot be equal for these persons (see the examples mentioned above). But justice means that the variable parameters compensate for the irreducible inequalities so that, finally, all the individual situations are equivalent to one another. The possibility of obtaining this result depends on the specific case and will be discussed below.

4 Justice and Partial Equity

The identity between equity and justice established for fundamental equity is no longer true for partial equity. Generally, *partial equity is unjust and justice is partially inequitable.*

Let us see this in the simplest case possible: a society
of two persons whose preferences are representable by
utility indices, bear upon a scalar variable which people
prefer to be higher (for example, a quantity of a consumed
good), and are differentiated by the value of a parameter of
any nature. Let the persons be labelled 1 and 2. Let x be
the variable (x_1 for individual 1 and x_2 for individual 2), λ
the parameter (λ_1 for individual 1 and λ_2 for individual 2),
and $u(\lambda, x)$ a specification of the common fundamental
utility index. Then

$$v_1(x) = u(\lambda_1, x)$$

$$v_2(x) = u(\lambda_2, x)$$

are specifications of the utility indices of individuals 1 and
2 for the partial problem. They are increasing functions of
x. The state (x_1, x_2) is [partially] equitable if

$$v_1(x_1) \geq v_1(x_2)$$

$$v_2(x_2) \geq v_2(x_1).$$

But these inequalities imply, respectively,

$$x_1 \geq x_2$$

$$x_2 \geq x_1.$$

A state is thus [partially] equitable if and only if $x_1 = x_2$.
On the other hand, in the just state [considering fundamental preferences] x_1 and x_2 satisfy

$$u(\lambda_1 , x_1) = u(\lambda_2 , x_2),$$

which requires in general $x_1 \neq x_2$ if $\lambda_1 \neq \lambda_2$.

This confirms that the deep meaning and value of partial equity is not global eudemonistic social ethics (the case of "justice"). They are, rather, the partial eleutheristic justice of equal freedom, for actual or potential choices in the ethically relevant settings. For example, the property of equity of free exchange, noted above, leaves aside any judgment involving the initial distribution. Indeed, if there is some inclusion of the initial distribution in the evaluation, free exchange can destroy equity: a bilateral exchange or a free market from an equitable initial distribution may give a final total allocation (initial distribution plus the quantities received and less the quantities given up) which is inequitable. Figure 25 shows an example of this in the case of two goods and two persons, with the analytical setting used in part 2. D_1 and D_2 are the curves of indifferent divisions of individuals 1 and 2, respectively, the area Q in between them is the locus of equitable allocations (border included), and the chosen initial allocation is the point of Q and of D_1 that is preferred by individual 2 (the indifference curve of individual 2 passing through this point, I_2, is tangent to D_1 at this point). Then, the allocations preferred to this initial allocation by individual 2 are not in Q and hence are no longer equitable, and free exchange from this starting point yields such an allocation.

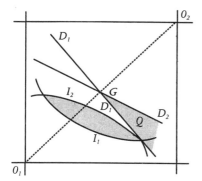

Figure 25

Hence a unanimous improvement from an equitable state, and in particular free exchange from equity, may yield an inequitable result: unanimous improvement or free exchange may destroy equity. But this cannot occur if the starting point is, moreover, efficient (the initial point chosen as the foregoing example is not on the locus of efficient points C). And the ethically important states are efficient and equitable and not only equitable.

On the other hand, fundamental equity, which is identical in its results to justice, attains preeminence from the point of view of overall eudemonistic justice. However, we will see that this concept often does not permit a resolution of the fundamental normative problem, which is the definition of the social optimum. Then it ceases to eclipse the other criteria, which can have an interest as second-best principles of eudemonistic justice. And among them, partial equity can play a role, in addition to its role of first-best principle for more partial issues valuing actual or hypothetical free choice.

5 Justice Can Be Inefficient or Impossible

One can, a priori, think that the optimum should be the best
possible just state. Unfortunately, the price to be paid, in
some way, for the fact that justice as it was defined is a
very deep concept on ethical grounds, is that it often does
not permit resolution of the problem. This depends on the
form of the domain of possible states. It could be that no
just state is possible (for example, if someone lost a leg, it
may be that no possible compensation could render him "as
happy" as someone who has all his limbs). Thus, *justice
can be impossible and life, necessarily, unjust.* If there are
possible just states, it is possible that the best of them is
inefficient, and, thus, that they all are inefficient (in the
preceding example, in fact, to cripple the others could
permit the establishment of justice, but the state obtained is
such that there was another possible state that was better for
some and worse for none). Thus, *justice can be inefficient
and efficiency necessarily unjust.* Since the optimum is by
definition possible and should certainly be efficient (see
section I.B.1), whatever its exact definition, *the optimum
may have to be unjust, and justice can be nonoptimal.*

Let us show the different cases again, using an example
that permits graphic representation. The society is composed of two persons (individuals 1 and 2), and we will
consider their two individual specifications of a specification of their fundamental utility. In a given state of society
let u_1 and u_2 be the levels of this index for individuals 1
and 2, respectively. To each state there corresponds a point
on a diagram in which u_1 and u_2 appear on the coordinate
axes (figure 26). The just states are such that $u_1 = u_2$, and,

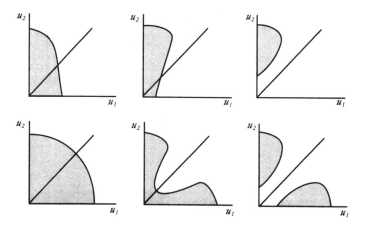

Figure 26

consequently, their locus is the first bisector of the axes. The hatched area $\wp$ represents the domain of possible states. The figure shows cases in which (a) there exists a possible just and efficient state, (b) there exist possible just states, but none is efficient, and (c) there does not exist a possible just state. The second line of diagrams shows that these three cases can occur even if it is always possible to permute the situations of the two persons, which means that $\wp$ is symmetric with respect to the first bisector of the axes (the locus of just states).

Hence, the concept of justice certainly cannot designate a best distribution of situations and goods to everyone in all cases. Moreover, the end value and ideal equalizand of social justice is not always individual satisfaction, happiness or welfare, and it is in certain cases various means of action such as liberties, rights, powers, incomes (purchasing power), or other goods. However, this concept of eudemonistic justice can contribute to the resolution of the general problem by application to more restricted groups of persons whose opportunities are comparable, differences compensable, and satisfactions more or less equalizable.

Besides, since the concept of fundamental equity, that is, justice, cannot be the universal solution for both empirical and moral reasons, it does not displace the concept of partial equity and it leads us to look for other noteworthy criteria that can be useful. Now, the idea of fundamental preference provides useful criteria even when the definition of justice based on this idea does not resolve the problem. They are *practical justice*, *adequacy* and its extensions and restrictions, *fundamental dominance*, *fundamental efficiency*, *fundamental majority*, *extremal majority*, *rank principles*, *comparisons of ordinal inequalities*, *truncations*, and so on. We will begin with adequacy, since the others all belong, in a sense, to the same family.

B Adequacy

1 Definition

The concept of adequacy is, in a certain sense, *dual* to that of equity. It arises from the consideration of fundamental preferences defined above. Roughly we will say that a state of society is adequate if each situation is attributed to the person who draws the most utility from it.[2]

Given a fundamental preference ordering, divide into two parts the set of traits that characterizes the state of a person: the one part, x, will be variable in the problem considered, and the other part, y, will be characteristic of this person in this problem. Let (x, y) designate the set of traits on which fundamental preference operates. Call x_i and y_i respectively, the x and y of individual i. Denote the relation of fundamental preference or indifference as $\succsim$. Individuals i and j are all the individuals in a defined society.

The set of x_i is *equitable* when

$$(x_i, y_i) \succeq (x_j, y_i) \text{ for all } i, j.$$

We will say that the set of the x_i is *adequate* when

---

2. Adequacy is related to the standard conception of justice in Antiquity (Plato, Aristotle): Each thing should be given to him who makes the best of it (e.g., "Give the flutes to the flute-player"). In a neighboring vein, Bertold Brecht said: "It is good that each thing belongs to whomever makes it better." Adequacy in a sense reverses this expression by saying, "It is good that each thing is given to whomever needs it most."

$$(x_i, y_i) \succeq (x_i, y_j) \text{ for all } i, j.$$

If fundamental preferences are representable by a utility index, let $u(x, y)$ be any of its specifications. Then, using the notation

$$u_j^i = u(x_j, y_i),$$

the set of x_i is *equitable* when

$$u_i^i \geq u_j^i \text{ for all } i, j,$$

and it is *adequate* when

$$u_i^i \geq u_i^j \text{ for all } i, j.$$

Equity and adequacy thus correspond to these properties of the square matrix of the u_j^i: the elements of the principal diagonal dominate in the rows in one case and in the columns in the other. Note that adequacy can always be defined in this manner because the individuals, and, thus, the pairs (x_i, y_j), are finite in number and, therefore, a preference ordering of them can always be represented using a utility index.

Various concepts of *realistic* and *restricted adequacy* can be defined as concepts of realistic equity have been.

Minimal adequacy is: For each i there is at least one $j \neq i$ such that $(x_i, y_i) \succeq (x_i, y_j)$ and $u_i^i \geq u_j^i$ (with strict $\succ$ and $>$ for *strict minimal adequacy*). The corresponding *realistic* and *restricted* concepts are defined as for equity.

2 Equity and Adequacy

Of course, a state of society can be equitable without being adequate and adequate without being equitable. But there exists a noteworthy relation between equity and adequacy. The relation is revealed when we compare states that are permuted from one another in the sense used in part I, that is, here, a set of n x_i and n y_i (i.e., of n individuals i) and *assignments* between the x_i on the one hand and the y_i on the other (in each assignment, each person has one and only one x_i, and each x_i is attributed to one and only one person). There is a total of $n!$ such assignments (permuted states), but we may consider only a sub-set of them (for instance, the ones that are possible).

We will begin by showing examples of possible situations and of impossible ones for the case $n = 2$.

$u_1^1 > u_2^1$
$\vee \qquad \vee$ No assignment is either equitable or adequate.
$u_1^2 > u_2^2$

$u_1^1 > u_2^1$
$\vee \qquad \vee$ One assignment is equitable but none is adequate.
$u_1^2 < u_2^2$

$u_1^1 > u_2^1$
$\vee \qquad \wedge$ One assignment is adequate but none is equitable.
$u_1^2 > u_2^2$

$$u_1^1 > u_2^1$$
$\lor \quad \land$ The same assignment is equitable and adequate.
$$u_1^2 < u_2^2$$

$$u_1^1 > u_2^1$$
$\land \quad \lor$ One assignment is equitable and the other is ade-
$$u_1^2 < u_2^2$$ quate.

The inequalities show that this last case is impossible.[3]

As a general rule, given a set of permuted states, several situations may occur. There may not exist any equitable or adequate states. There may exist one or more that are equitable and none that is adequate. Also, there may exist one or more that are adequate and none that is equitable. But, we will show that if there is only one equitable state and only one adequate state, it is necessarily the same state. More generally, we will show that there is, between equity and adequacy, the following relation (in which "one" means "at least one").

Theorem
If, among permuted states, there is one equitable state and there is one adequate state, all the states that have one property also have the other.

In order to prove this theorem, consider a set of n persons, that is, of $n\, y_i$, and of $n\, x_i$ ($i = 1, 2, ..., n$). Then consider the various *assignments* of these x_i to these

---

3. *Translator's note*: That is, it violates transitivity.

individuals. Any two of these assignments are social states (defined by the set of assigned x_i) permuted from one another. There are in total $n!$ assignments. Define again u_j^i as a utility index representing the fundamental preference for (x_j, y_i) (since the number of distinct pairs (x_j, y_i) is finite, the fundamental preferences about them can always be represented by such an index). For each assignment there corresponds a set of n numbers $\{u_j^i\}$, in which the sets of the i and of the j are permutations of the n integers.

Among the various possible proofs of the theorem, one (particularly revealing) considers any *symmetric* and *increasing* real valued function of these n numbers, $M = M(u_{j_1}^1, u_{j_2}^2, ..., u_{j_n}^n)$. The symmetry means that M does not change when the arguments are permuted. M could, for instance, be the sum or the product of these numbers. We will later see an interesting social interpretation of such a function.

Let α and β denote *permutations* of the first n integers. $\alpha(i)$ and $\beta(i)$ are the numbers in the respective permutations that correspond to the integer i. There is one-to-one correspondence between the permutations α, the assignments $(x_{\alpha(i)}, y_i)$, and the sets

$$u_{\alpha(1)}^1, u_{\alpha(2)}^2, ..., u_{\alpha(n)}^n.$$

We will say that a permutation α or β is equitable or adequate when the state created by the corresponding assignment is equitable or adequate (recall that inequitable and inadequate mean non-equitable and non-adequate). Finally, write (without risk of ambiguity)

$$M(\alpha) = M(u^1_{\alpha(1)}, u^2_{\alpha(2)}, ..., u^n_{\alpha(n)}).$$

We first will show a series of relations between M and equity.

1. If α and β are equitable, $M(\alpha) = M(\beta)$. Indeed, we then have for each i

$$u^i_{\alpha(i)} \geq u^i_{\beta(i)}$$

and

$$u^i_{\beta(i)} \geq u^i_{\alpha(i)},$$

from which it follows that

$$u^i_{\alpha(i)} = u^i_{\beta(i)}$$

and thus

$$M(\alpha) = M(\beta).$$

2. If α is equitable and β inequitable, $M(\alpha) > M(\beta)$. Indeed, we then have for each i

$$u^i_{\alpha(i)} \geq u^i_{\beta(i)};$$

all if

$$u^i_{\alpha(i)} = u^i_{\beta(i)}$$

for all i, β would be equitable. Thus,

$$u^i_{\alpha(i)} > u^i_{\beta(i)}$$

for at least one i. Consequently,

$$M(\alpha) > M(\beta).$$

3. If α is equitable and $M(\alpha) = M(\beta)$, β is equitable. Indeed, if β were inequitable, according to property 2 we would have $M(\alpha) > M(\beta)$.

4. If α is equitable and $M(\alpha) > M(\beta)$, β is inequitable. Indeed, if β were equitable, according to property 1 we would have $M(\alpha) = M(\beta)$.

These four properties are summarized as follows: α being equitable, β is equitable if and only if $M(\alpha) = M(\beta)$, and β is inequitable if and only if $M(\alpha) > M(\beta)$. Consequently, if there exist at least one equitable permuted state, the set of the equitable states and the set of the states in which M takes its maximum value are identical.

We now will show that the same property holds for adequacy, using similar reasonings and the symmetry of the function M. Now α and β represent permutations of subscripts into superscripts. We use the same identification among a permutation α, the assignment $(x_i, y_{\alpha(i)})$ and the set of numbers $u_i^{\alpha(i)}$, for $i = 1, ..., n$. There exist the following relations between M and adequacy.

1. If α and β are adequate, $M(\alpha) = M(\beta)$. Indeed, we then have for each i

$$u_i^{\alpha(i)} \geq u_i^{\beta(i)}$$

and

$$u_i^{\beta(i)} \geq u_i^{\alpha(i)},$$

and therefore,

$$u_i^{\alpha(i)} = u_i^{\beta(i)}.$$

These u_i^j thus constitute two groups of n numbers each, such that for each number in one group there corresponds, in a one-to-one fashion, an equal number in the other group. M is a function of these groups of numbers that, by the definition of symmetry, does not depend on the order of the numbers. The M's of these two groups are, therefore, equal.

2. If α is adequate and β is inadequate, $M(\alpha) > M(\beta)$. Indeed, we then have for each i

$$u_i^{\alpha(i)} \geq u_i^{\beta(i)};$$

and if

$$u_i^{\alpha(i)} = u_i^{\beta(i)}$$

for each i, β would be adequate. Thus,

$$u_i^{\alpha(i)} > u_i^{\beta(i)}$$

for at least one i. These u_i^j thus constitute two groups of n numbers each such that to each number of the second there corresponds in a one-to-one fashion a number of the first that is not smaller and, in at least one case, is larger. M is a function of these groups that does not depend on the order of the numbers. It is, moreover, an increasing function of its arguments. We thus have $M(\alpha) > M(\beta)$.

3. If α is adequate and $M(\alpha) = M(\beta)$, β is adequate. Indeed, if β were inadequate, according to property 2 we would have $M(\alpha) > M(\beta)$.

4. If α is adequate and $M(\alpha) > M(\beta)$, β is inadequate. Indeed, if β were adequate, according to property 1 we would have $M(\alpha) = M(\beta)$.

These four properties are summarized as follows: α being adequate, β is adequate if and only if $M(\alpha) = M(\beta)$, and β is inadequate if and only if $M(\alpha) > M(\beta)$. Consequently, if there exists at least one adequate permuted state, the set of the adequate states and the set of the states in which M takes its maximum value are identical.

The theorem is proved by the two final relations obtained between M and, on the one hand, equity, and, on the other hand, adequacy.

More generally, a similar result holds for *"restricted" equity and adequacy* defined by the equity and adequacy comparisons only between pairs of permuted states taken from a subset R of the $n!$ permuted states. This can in particular be realistic equity and adequacy if the set R is the set of possible permuted states and this "realism" is so defined. Full equity and adequacy are the particular cases where the set R encompasses all the $n!$ permuted states. More precisely, restricted (and notably realistic) equity and adequacy relative to a set R, denoted as R-equity and R-adequacy, are respectively defined as follows: P_R denoting the set of n-permutations corresponding to the assignments of the n x_j to the n y_i in R, and assuming by notation that $P_R \in 1$ where 1 denotes the unit permutation ($j = i$), then the state $\{(x_i, y_i)\}$ is R-equitable when $(x_i, y_i) \succsim (x_{\pi(i)}, y_i)$ for all $\pi \in P_R$, and it is R-adequate when $(x_i, y_i) \succsim (x_i, y_{\pi^{-1}(i)})$ for all $\pi \in P_R$.

Then, the theorem is that if, in the set R, there exists at least one R-equitable state and at least one R-adequate state, any state in R that has one of these properties also has the other. One proof straightforwardly duplicates the preceding one in considering only permutations in P_R, and in considering the maximum of the function M in the set R. Another property of R-equitable and R-adequate states, and another proof, will be shown when "fundamental dominance" will be introduced (section III.C.4.h.).

Remark[4]

It is noteworthy that the theorem does not hold true if the number of persons n is infinite rather than finite. The following example of infinite matrix u_j^i shows this: for all

---

4. I owe this remark to Edmond Baudier.

integers m, $u_m^m = 2m - 1$, $u_{m+1}^m = 2m$, and $u_j^i = 0$ in all other cases.

1	2	0	0	0	...
0	3	4	0	0	...
0	0	5	6	0	...
0	0	0	7	8	...

(For this structure to hold, the increasing u_j^i need not become infinite: they can tend toward an asymptotic value.)

C Fundamentalism

1 Presentation

a Intention

We will now define and study new properties based on the *use of fundamental preferences in order to compare states of society two by two.* This comparison will consist in saying that one of the two considered states is better than the other or that they are equivalent. But the final problem always is to define the best of the possible states, i.e., to designate the optimum. The help that this binary relation brings to the resolution of the problem depends on its structure and on the set of possible states. In certain cases the relation will resolve the problem; in the others it will contribute to the solution by eliminating states that are inferior to other possible ones, that is, by limiting the set of states among which one should look for the optimum.

We will study several of these criteria, their properties, the relations among them, and their relations with properties previously studied (efficiency, justice, equity, adequacy).

b Bases of the Criteria

These criteria will have as a characteristic that *the comparison between two states of society depends exclusively on the members' preferences between these two states.*

Let us specify that these individual preferences are only "I prefer the one to the other or I am indifferent," without any consideration of something that would resemble an intensity of preference. In other words, since we still consider these individuals to be "rational" in the economists' sense, i.e., each individual's preferences among the states of society constitute an "ordering," only these individual preference orderings will be used to compare the states. (This condition also has been respected in all the properties studied above.) This consideration of individuals' preference orderings only is a great strength of the approach. Moreover, the noted characteristic adds also that the comparisons between two states of society will depend only on individual preferences *between these two states*, and in no way on properties of these preferences which consider other states. It is the property that Kenneth Arrow called "independence of irrelevant alternatives."[5]

The fact that the comparisons between states depend solely on individuals' preference comparisons can mean several things, and it can be a choice or a necessity, depending on the definition of a state and on the interpretation of a preference. A state can be an "end-state" (in general with items at several dates: this is a concept in the logic of action and causality rather than one referring only to time). But its description can also include that of processes, rules, means, rights, powers, and so on. Individuals can value such elements solely by their "final" consequences, or they can in addition value them for other reasons. In the former case, these elements can be judged through the description, in a social state, of these consequences only, as a result of the considered exclusive reliance on individuals' preferences (which precludes the a

---

5. *Cf.* K. J. Arrow, *Social Choice and Individual Values* (Wiley, 1951).

priori social value of equal rights or equal means). Preferences can be understood as representing individuals' ends,
choices, happiness, pleasure, welfare, opinions, etc.—these
entities can be very different ones—, and they can refer to
one criterion of evaluation or to one type of criteria (such
as self-centered welfare or moral judgment), or to the
individuals' synthesis of various criteria. All this and the
following is consistent with the above definition of fundamental preferences (satisfaction can be the individual's end,
in particular the objective of her choices, it can be obtained
by conformity of the social state with the individual's
evaluative opinion, etc.).

Then, the dependence of comparisons on individuals'
preferences only can represent a social ethic of eudemonism, hedonism, or welfarism.[6] It can manifest an individ-
ualistic social ethic that thoroughly respects the individual
in end-valuing only individuals' ends (rather than certain of
their means) or choices, or in judging the world only
through individuals' views. These positions imply and
justify a "respect of individuals' preferences": unanimous
indifference implies social ethical indifference, unanimous
preference implies "better" (including if certain individuals
but not all are indifferent). Finally and in all generality,
since the reasons retained for finding one state preferable to
another are defended by individuals (the ethical theorist is
one of them), there is a sense in which such a judgment can
depend only on individuals' preferences properly defined.

---

6. *Translator's note*: See John Hicks, *Essays in World Economy*,
preface (Basil Blackwell, Oxford, 1959).

c Logic of the Criteria

α Binary Relations

The above concerns the foundation and the raw material of
the relations among states of society. The relations themselves will compare the states two by two as mentioned.
When the problem posed is limited to choosing between
two states of society, this may be sufficient for resolution.
But most often the possible states are more numerous.
These pairwise comparisons then introduce us to the field
of the logic of binary relations. This topic is classic and is
presented in many places; but more or less different
properties and structures can be used as basic concepts;
furthermore, the various authors use significantly different
vocabularies, denoting the same things differently and using
the same terms for different concepts; finally, only some of
the noteworthy properties and structures will be of interest
here.   Let us, therefore, briefly present the relations,
properties, structures and sets that will be useful, with our
definitions.

The relations operate on elements, which in our applications are states of society. Denote certain elements as a, b,
and c, and denote a binary relation R between a and b as
$a\,R\,b$.   All the properties stated will be for a, b, or c
belonging to a given defined set.

The useful properties of the relations are the following:

Transitivity: $a\,R\,b$ and $b\,R\,c \Rightarrow a\,R\,c$

Symmetry: $a\,R\,b \Rightarrow b\,R\,a$

Antisymmetry: $a R b \Rightarrow$ not $b R a$

Completeness: for any pair of elements a and b of the set,
$a R b$ or $b R a$ (or both).

The noteworthy relations that will be useful are defined as follows:

Transitivity and symmetry: *equivalence*,

Transitivity: *ordering*,

Transitivity and antisymmetry: *strict ordering.*[7]

With an ordering relation R there are associated an equivalence relation I and a strict ordering relation S defined as:

$a I b \Leftrightarrow a R b$ and $b R a$,

$a S b \Leftrightarrow a R b$ and not $b R a$.

Given an equivalence relation, the set of elements equivalent to an element by this relation is called an *equivalence class*.

An element a is a *maximal element* of an ordering relation R if there does not exist an element b such that

---

7. *Author's note of 1997*: Ordering and strict ordering are also often denoted as preordering and ordering, respectively.

b S a. The existence of maximal elements requires properties of closure of the set of elements with regard to the relation, but, for the problems considered here, these properties can always be assumed.

Finally, one can easily verify the following properties which will be of great use. Let *S* and *I*, respectively, be the strict ordering and the equivalence relations associated with a *complete* ordering *R*. Then, the maximal elements of *R* constitute an equivalence class of *I*, and for any *a* that is a maximal element of *R* and any *b* that is not a maximal element of *R*, *a S b*.

β *The Logic of the Problem*
But our problem is to find the optimum among the possible states of society. How can a binary relation solve this problem or aid in solving it?

This problem would be solved if an ethically incontestable binary relation indicated that one possible state is better than each of the other possible states. We also could be satisfied by a relation that would indicate that several equivalent possible states are each better than every other possible state: the optimum would be any one of these states, and it would not matter which one were chosen. However, one may find it a virtue of this relation that it also satisfy certain properties when it is applied to other states, as in particular transitivity—which has a certain aspect of logical consistency—, although transitivity and completeness are unnecessary requirements, and hence excessive ones, when the problem is to select the optimum in a possibility set which is unique for the type of alternatives considered (for instance the global, overall, and intertemporal optimum to be chosen in the set of possible all-encompassing social states).

At any rate, the problem will be solved if one can find a relation of complete ordering with respect to which the domain of possible states is closed. Below, we will propose one complete ordering called "practical justice." But its moral relevance will not be general, in contrast to propositions of only partial orderings and the associated equivalences.

In certain cases, depending largely on the domain of possible states in the specific problem posed, a partial ordering can suffice to solve the problem insofar as it designates a single possible state or several equivalent possible states as better than each of the other possible states. But, in general, a partial ordering does not provide this result, and thus does not completely solve the problem. It, however, defines a set of states that are the maximal elements of the ordering on the domain of possible states: each such element is a possible state and is such that no better state is possible. These states are not all equivalent to one another. But, we know that the optimum is one of them if one endorses the criterion defined by the relation. Additional criteria are necessary to determine which one it is. But the relation, nevertheless, will have been useful because it will have limited the set of states among which we must continue this quest for optimality. Such a relation will a priori be the more useful the more it restricts this set of candidates for the optimum.

d Notations

In order to present and analyze the new criteria, which depend in an essential way on the consideration of fundamental preferences, we will need the very classic criteria founded on unanimity and in no way requiring fundamental preferences. We will review these criteria in order to define well those aspects that are important here, to note them in the framework of the present notations and concepts, and to present some useful comments. But, in order not to multiply notations, we will do this directly with the concepts of fundamental preferences that will be indispensable in what follows. We will thus begin by giving a first wave of notations in which fundamental preferences are present, then we will use them to analyze the criteria of unanimity without any intervention of the fact that the individual preferences are fundamental. We will then concentrate on the consequences of "fundamentalism." This will impose new notations that will be used subsequently for the definition and analysis of various "fundamental properties": fundamental unanimity, practical justice, the various fundamental and extremal majorities and rank principles, comparisons of ordinal inequalities and truncations, etc.

Let us give the first notations.

The society being considered is composed of n members of index i: $i = 1, 2, ..., n$, where $n \geq 2$. These i will be the only ones considered, thus we will not repeat that they are members of this society.

Denote as z the exhaustive set of traits characterizing the situation of a person when we consider fundamental preferences as ranking specifications of z, in the society being considered (see sections I.A.4 and III.A.1).

Let z_i be the specification of z corresponding to a state of individual i.

A state of society is entirely defined by a description of the situations of all its members, that is, by the specification of a z_i for each i. This state is thus represented by the set Z of the n z_i:

$$Z = \{z_1, z_2, ..., z_n\}.$$

Z completely describes the state of society for all practical purposes, and judgments comparing the states of society bear upon various specifications of Z. They will be denoted as Z, Z', Z'', etc., and z_i, z_i', z_i'' will denote the corresponding z_i.

We always denote the relations of fundamental preferences as follows: $\succ$ for preference, $\sim$ for equivalence and $\succsim$ for $\succ$ or $\sim$. They compare various z two by two. The ordering relation $\succsim$ is complete in the domain of Z considered.

When this relation is representable by an ordinal utility index, $u(z)$ denotes any given specification of this index, and it will be called the fundamental utility index. Let us then write $u_i = u(z_i)$, and denote the vector of n u_i as U. U is a function of Z, $U(Z)$. Intuitive understanding can be helped by graphic representations in the space of U in the case where $n = 2$, with two coordinate axes bearing respectively u_1 and u_2. Denoted $u_i' = u(z_i')$, $u_i'' = u(z_i'')$, and U' and U'' as the vectors of u_i' and u_i'': thus, $U' = U(Z')$ and $U'' = U(Z'')$. Classical vector notations

are used: $U = U'$ for $u_i = u'_i$ for all i, $U \geqq U'$ for $u_i \geq u'_i$
for all i, and $U \geq U'$ for $u_i \geq u'_i$ for all i and $u_i > u'_i$ for at
least one i.

When the problem is to compare a finite number of Z
(it will be two or three), n being finite, the total number of
specifications of z considered is finite: it is n times this
number of Z. Then, the fundamental preference between
these elements can always be represented by a fundamental
utility index.   It would be the same if a denumerable
infinity of Z were considered. But domains of possible Z
that can include a non-denumerable infinity of Z will also
be considered. Then, u may not exist. This is why the
considered properties will be defined and studied with
fundamental preference orderings rather than only with a
fundamental utility index, but they will also in general be
repeated for the case in which u does exist (in particular
because this will permit graphic illustrations).   One may
add that in practice the individual's sensitivity threshold
may very well be such that it is sufficient, for all useful
purposes, to consider a denumerable infinity, or probably
even a finite number, of specifications of z. In the following, when we refer to u, or u_i, or U, or to concepts that are
deduced from them (they will be defined later), it is implicitly understood that these are cases in which this fundamental utility index exists.

Let us note here that all the concepts and results
presented below hold if one only and directly uses ordinal
interpersonally comparable functions u_i of the state of the
world. This would indeed be a better specification of the
problem if the considered preferences had an extended
scope (including, for example, external effects, moral

judgments, and so on). Then, no variable z_i has to be considered. However, the analysis will be presented here with z_i so as to relate it to a number of applications and of comparisons with other criteria (notably with $z_i = (x_i, y_i)$ with the concepts of previous sections).

Finally, the set (domain) of possible Z will be denoted as P, and the set (domain) of possible U will be denoted *as* $\mathcal{P}$. By definition of $\mathcal{P}$, $Z \in P \Rightarrow U(Z) \in \mathcal{P}$, and for any $U \in \mathcal{P}$ there exists at least one $Z \in P$ such that $U = U(Z)$. The completeness of relations that will be considered refers to the set P.

2 Unanimity

The first classical properties announced are the following. They derive from the fact, discussed above, that comparisons of states of society depend only on the preferences of the members of the society. These relations will be called *unanimous equivalence, unanimous preference, and unanimous preference or equivalence*. They lead to the property of *efficiency*.

Let us use the following notations:

$Z(UE)Z'$: Z is unanimously equivalent to Z'.

$Z(UP)Z'$: Z is unanimously preferred to Z'.

$Z(UPE)Z'$: Z is unanimously preferred or equivalent to Z'.

These relations are defined thus:

$$Z(UE)Z' \iff z_i \sim z'_i \text{ for all } i.$$

$$Z(UP)Z' \iff \begin{cases} z_i \succsim z'_i \text{ for all } i \\ \text{and} \\ z_i \succ z'_i \text{ for at least one } i. \end{cases}$$

$$Z(UPE)Z' \iff z_i \succsim z'_i \text{ for all } i.$$

(Another concept of unanimous preference, $z_i \succ z'_i$ for all i, will not be useful here.) These relations obviously have the following properties: all three are *transitive*; unanimous equivalence is *symmetric*; and unanimous preference is *antisymmetric*. Consequently, unanimous equivalence is an *equivalence relation*. It thus defines equivalence classes that will be called *unanimous equivalence classes*. Unanimous preference is a *strict ordering*. Unanimous preference or equivalence (*UPE*) is an *ordering*. We have

$$Z(UPE)Z' \iff Z(UE)Z' \text{ or } Z(UP)Z'$$

$$Z(UE)Z' \iff Z(UPE)Z' \text{ and } Z'(UPE)Z$$

$$Z(UP)Z' \iff \begin{cases} Z(UPE)Z' \text{ and not } Z'(UPE)Z \\ \text{that is,} \\ Z(UPE)Z' \text{ and not } Z(UE)Z'. \end{cases}$$

Unanimous equivalence and unanimous preference are, respectively, the equivalence relation and the strict ordering that are associated with unanimous preference or equivalence. The "laws of composition" of these three relations, two by two, are obvious.

We also have

$$Z(UE)Z' \iff U = U'$$

$$Z(UP)Z' \iff U \geq U'$$

$$Z(UPE)Z' \iff U \geqq U'.$$

The first of these properties shows that there is a one-to-one correspondence between the classes of unanimous equivalence and the vectors U.

None of the three relations is, in general, *complete* (it would be sufficient that unanimous equivalence (UE) or unanimous preference (UP) be complete, for unanimous preference or equivalence (UPE) to be complete). In order for them to be complete, the domain of possible states must have very particular structures. Thus, unanimous equivalence is complete only if $\mathcal{P}$ is reduced to a point (figure 27(a)); unanimous preference or equivalence is complete only in the case in which the form of $\mathcal{P}$ is like that in figure 27(b); and unanimous preference is complete only in this case and if, in addition, to each $U \in \mathcal{P}$ there corresponds a single Z.

One may consider that, when they are complete, these relations are sufficient to solve the problem because then there is a possible state, or a set of equivalent possible states,

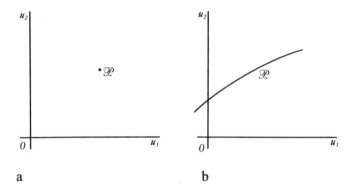

Figure 27

that is (are) better than all other possible states (these other
possible states do not exist for unanimous equivalence).
But this property can be the case even without the relations
being complete, for unanimous preference and unanimous
preference or equivalence. Then, this property holds even
though there are pairs of possible states between which the
relation does not establish any comparison. Obviously,
these pairs include no state better than or equivalent to all
the other possible states. The existence of this possibility
depends on the structure of the domain of possible states.
Figures 28(a) and 28(b) show examples for the case of
unanimous preference or equivalence. The possible Z such
that $U(Z) = U^*$ are equivalent to one another and each is
unanimously preferred to each of the other possible states.
But among these other possible states there exist pairs of

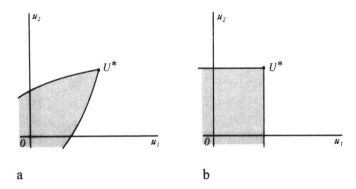

a   b

Figure 28

incomparable states. The same structure of possible states
yields the same conclusion for unanimous preference if, in
addition, there exists only a single possible Z such that
$U(Z) = U^*$.

In the general case, these relations, even if they do not
solve the problem, can contribute to its solution. Indeed,
they limit the search for the optimum to the maximal
elements of the relation of unanimous preference, that is, to
the possible states such that no possible state is unanimously preferred to any of them. These states are none other
than the *efficient* states. Precisely, Z is efficient if $Z \in P$
and if there is no state $Z' \in P$ such that $Z'(UP)Z$. These
efficient states are the ones that correspond to the maximal
elements of the relation $\geq$ on the $U \in \mathcal{P}$ (figure 29).

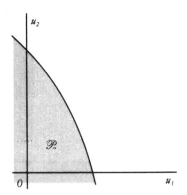

Figure 29

Generally there are several efficient states and they are not unanimously equivalent to one another. The exceptions are the cases noted above. Seeking the optimum among these efficient states runs into the difficulty that there are too many of them. Consequently, we should find ways to further reduce the set of admissible states. Now, there is a property that the preceding criteria did not exploit: the consideration of fundamental preference. It offers a new and rich field of possibilities.

3 Permutation and Ordered States

a Permutation Equivalence

With the concepts utilized here, a person is entirely defined by her situation and her preferences. With fundamental preferences, individuals have the same preferences. Thus, they are distinguishable from one another only by their situations, that is, owing to the z that are attributed to them. In other words, if z is variable, individuals are distinguished only by their preferences, but because the preferences are fundamental, the individuals no longer are distinguishable at all. As a result, a different assignment of the n specifications z_i of z among the individuals yields a state of society that is indistinguishable from the first from the standpoint of judgment among states of society. This assignment amounts to choosing the order of classification of these n specifications of z. Thus, for normative purposes, the state of society is characterized only by the nonordered set of the n z_i.

In particular, Z is necessarily "socially equivalent" to Z' if the series $z_1, z_2, ..., z_n$ and $z'_1, z'_2, ..., z'_n$ are permutations (without omission or repetition) of one another. We say in this case that Z is a *permuted* state of Z', or that Z and Z' are permuted states of one another. The property of equivalence of these Z and Z' will be called *permutation equivalence*. Since permutation is a symmetric relation (if Z is a permuted state of Z', Z' is a permuted state of Z) and a transitive relation (if Z is a permuted state of Z' and Z' is a permuted state of Z'', Z is a permuted state of Z''), the same is true of this normative comparison among states of society: it constitutes an *equivalence relation*, and it defines *equivalence classes* in which all the states are permuted from one another.

Remark
The preceding relates to the problem of comparing states, not to the complete problem that also introduces the domain of possible states. A permuted state of a possible state may

be impossible: individuals may intervene in a nonsym-
metric way in the domain of possible states. We have even
seen that this risks being more the case the more one
extends the domain of the considered traits of individual
situations in including individual characteristics, a process
that one extends quite far in considering fundamental
preferences. That is why we have not said that two
permuted states are, for all practical purposes, *identical*, but
only that they are *equivalent* for purposes of "social
judgment": they can differ with regard to their inclusion in
or exclusion from the domain of possible states.

b Ordered States

In each of the permutation equivalence classes we now will
choose a representative element. This will be a state of
society for which the z_i are ordered by the nondecreasing
fundamental preference ordering. We will call it an
ordered state of its class, that is, of its permuted states. In
other words, an ordered state of a state $Z = \{z_1, z_2, ..., z_n\}$
is a state $Z_0 = \{\zeta_1, \zeta_2, ..., \zeta_n\}$ such that:

1. Z_0 is a permuted state of Z, and

2. $\zeta_i \precsim \zeta_{i+1}$ for all $i = 1, 2, ..., n - 1$.

Z_0 is also an ordered state of all the permuted states of Z.
If for no pair of indices i, j different from one another, we
have $z_i \sim z_j$, there is only one ordered state of Z and
$\zeta_i \prec \zeta_{i+1}$ for all $i = 1, 2, ..., n - 1$. If not, there are several

ordered states of Z, but any one of them will serve equally well for what follows.

Because of permutation equivalence, all the properties of Z that are relevant in order to judge the states of society also belong to its ordered states. For this purpose we can thus substitute one of them for Z.

Denote

$$v_i = u(\zeta_i).$$

In other words, the v_i are the u_i classified by a nondecreasing order. We also will write $v_i = v(i)$, which defines a function v of i. The representative curve of this function we will call the *curve of ordered utilities*. This function is nondecreasing since $v_i \leq v_{i+1}$ for $i = 1, 2, ..., n - 1$ (figure 30). It is strictly increasing if and only if there is only a single ordered state of Z. These properties remain when u is replaced by an increasing function of u, as they should since u is only an ordinal index. The same will have to be true for any other properties involving such curves.

All states permuted from one another have the same curve of ordered utilities.

c *Just States*

Note the particular properties of *just* states with respect to the properties just discussed. In a just state, by definition all the z_i are equivalent to one another for the fundamental preferences. Therefore, a permuted state of a just state also is just. This state and all its permuted states are ordered states of their permutation equivalence class. All the u_i and

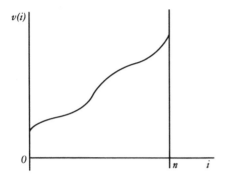

Figure 30

all the v_i are equal, and the curve of ordered utilities is
horizontal (figure 31); reciprocally, such a curve is the
mark of a just state. Moreover, a permuted state of a just
state is unanimously equivalent to it. Thus, a class of
permutation equivalent just states is included in a class of
unanimously equivalent just states.

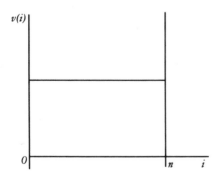

Figure 31

With $n = 2$, the locus of the U of just states is the first bisector of the axes (figure 32). Two states permuted from one another have symmetric U with respect to this line.

Denote as Z_0', ζ_i', $v'(i)$, and Z_0'', ζ_i'', $v''(i)$, as the Z_0, ζ_i, $v(i)$ corresponding to Z' and Z'', respectively. Also, denote the state of Z transformed by a permutation π as πZ, denote the inverse of π as π^{-1}, and let π' denote another permutation. Recall that identity is a permutation, and that the product of two permutations is a permutation. Call the permutation π, such that $Z_0 = \pi Z$, an *ordering permutation*. Permutation equivalence, associated with the criteria of unanimity, leads to noteworthy properties.

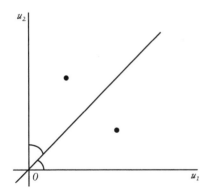

Figure 32

*

4 Fundamental Equivalence and Dominance

a *Fundamental Equivalence*

Unanimous equivalence and permutation equivalence yield *fundamental equivalence*. Fundamental equivalence can be defined by any of the equivalent properties that will be pointed out. Let us choose, for instance, that by definition, *states of society are fundamentally equivalent if their ordered states are unanimously equivalent.*

Write $Z(FE)Z'$ for "Z is fundamentally equivalent to Z'," and define

$$Z(FE)Z' \Leftrightarrow Z_0(UE)Z_0'.$$

The properties of unanimous equivalence and the definition of ordered states readily show that

$$Z(FE)Z' \Leftrightarrow Z'(FE)Z,$$

$$Z(FE)Z' \text{ and } Z'(FE)Z'' \Rightarrow Z(FE)Z'',$$

that is, this binary relation is *symmetric* and *transitive*. It is, therefore, an *equivalence relation*. Call its equivalence classes *fundamental equivalence classes*. This justifies the vocabulary used and the verbal definition given.

Clearly, states are fundamentally equivalent if and only if they have the same curve of ordered utilities. There is, thus, one-to-one correspondence between the curves of ordered utilities and the fundamental equivalence classes.

For $n = 2$, a fundamental equivalence class is the set of states of which the U are one or the other of two symmetric points with respect to the first bisector of the axes (see figure 32). As limiting cases, these two points merge on this line and all these states are just.

The following three properties also hold; the first two are characteristic and thus can define fundamental equivalence.

1. *Two states are fundamentally equivalent if and only if there exist a permuted state of one and a permuted state of the other that are unanimously equivalent.*

Indeed, if $Z(FE)Z'$ then it is sufficient to use Z_0 and Z_0' for those permuted states and we have $Z_0(UE)Z_0'$. And if there exist π and π' such that $\pi Z(UE)\pi'Z'$, then πZ and $\pi'Z'$ have the same ordered states, but since they each have the same ordered states as Z and Z', Z and Z' also have the same ordered states, and $Z(FE)Z'$.

2. *Two states are fundamentally equivalent if and only if one is unanimously equivalent to a permuted state of the other.*

Since identity is a particular permutation, the sufficient condition is a corollary of property 1. And if $Z(FE)Z'$, call π and π' ordering permutations: $Z_0 = \pi Z$ and $Z_0' = \pi'Z'$. Then, $Z_0(UE)Z_0'$ writes $\pi Z(UE)\pi'Z'$, which implies both, $Z(UE)\pi^{-1}\pi'Z'$ and $\pi'^{-1}\pi Z(UE)Z'$. Hence, the property is proved, but it should of course be stated more precisely in saying that if two states are fundamentally equivalent, each is unanimously equivalent to a permuted state of the other.

3. *Unanimous equivalence implies fundamental equivalence.*

This is a corollary of the sufficient conditions of properties 1 and 2, since identity is a particular permutation. It follows from this that unanimous equivalence classes are subsets of fundamental equivalence classes.

b Fundamental Dominance

Unanimous preference and permutation equivalence yield *fundamental dominance*. Fundamental dominance can be defined by any of the equivalent properties that will be pointed out. Let us choose, for instance, that by definition, *a state of society fundamentally dominates another if its ordered states are unanimously preferred to those of the other.* One can easily verify that the relation does not depend on the particular ordered states chosen when they are not unique.

Let us write $Z(FD)Z'$ for "Z fundamentally dominates Z'." The definition is

$$Z(FD)Z' \Leftrightarrow Z_0(UP)Z'_0.$$

In other words,

$$Z(FD)Z' \iff \begin{cases} \zeta_i \gtrsim \zeta_i' \text{ for all } i \\ \\ \text{and} \\ \\ \zeta_i \succ \zeta_i' \text{ for at least one } i. \end{cases}$$

Or,

$$Z(FD)Z' \iff \begin{cases} v_i \geq v_i' \text{ for all } i \\ \\ \text{and} \\ \\ v_i > v_i' \text{ for at least one } i. \end{cases}$$

This last form shows that the fact that one state fundamentally dominates another is represented by that state's curve of ordered utilities being nowhere below, and in certain places above, that of the other (figure 33).

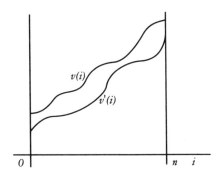

Figure 33

These last relations are, as they have to be, purely ordinal in the sense that they do not change when u is replaced by any increasing function of u.

The application of the properties of unanimous preference to Z_0 shows that fundamental dominance also satisfies these properties. Fundamental dominance, therefore, is *transitive* and *antisymmetric*:

$$Z(FD)Z' \text{ and } Z'(FD)Z'' \Rightarrow Z(FD)Z''$$

$$Z(FD)Z' \Rightarrow \text{not } Z'(FD)Z.$$

It is thus a relation of *strict ordering*.

Fundamental dominance satisfies the following "law of composition" with fundamental equivalence:

$$Z(FE)Z' \text{ and } Z'(FD)Z'' \Rightarrow Z(FD)Z''$$

$$Z(FD)Z' \text{ and } Z'(FE)Z'' \Rightarrow Z(FD)Z''.$$

Also define the relation of *fundamental dominance or equivalence*. Write $Z(FDE)Z'$ for "Z fundamentally dominates Z' or is fundamentally equivalent to Z'." By definition,

$$Z(FDE)Z' \Leftrightarrow Z_0(UPE)Z_0'$$

$$Z(FDE)Z' \Leftrightarrow Z(FD)Z' \text{ or } Z(FE)Z'$$

$$Z(FDE)Z' \Leftrightarrow \zeta_i \succsim \zeta_i' \text{ for all } i$$

$$Z(FDE)Z' \Leftrightarrow v_i \geq v'_i \text{ for all } i.$$

This last form shows that $Z(FDE)Z'$ is equivalent to having the curve of ordered utilities of Z "nowhere below" that of Z'; it is an ordinal property in the sense indicated.

It is readily seen that the relation of fundamental dominance or equivalence is *transitive*. It is not symmetric (if a particular form of the domain of possible states does not reduce it to fundamental equivalence). It thus constitutes an *ordering* relation. One can straightforwardly write the laws of composition of fundamental dominance or equivalence with, respectively, fundamental dominance and fundamental equivalence. Finally, we have

$$Z(FE)Z' \Leftrightarrow Z(FDE)Z' \text{ and } Z'(FDE)Z,$$

$$Z(FD)Z' \Leftrightarrow Z(FDE)Z' \text{ and not } Z(FE)Z',$$

that is, fundamental equivalence and fundamental dominance are, respectively, the relations of equivalence and of strict ordering associated with fundamental dominance or equivalence. (One other relation of the same family, which would be $\zeta_i > \zeta'_i$ for all i, will not be useful here.)

But these three relations generally are *not complete*. Indeed, since the relations based on unanimity are not complete, they are in particular not complete on the ordered states. This property really is noteworthy only for fundamental dominance or equivalence (and fundamental dominance or equivalence would be complete if either fundamental dominance or fundamental equivalence were complete). We can have neither $Z(FDE)Z'$ nor $Z'(FDE)Z$.

In this case the curves of ordered utilities of Z and Z' intersect in at least one point (figure 34). These relations are complete only for particular forms of the domain of possible states, such as those shown on figure 27, or those that add to $\mathcal{P}$ the symmetric to the $\mathcal{P}$ of the figure with respect to the first bisector of the axes, with a discussion similar to that presented for the unanimity properties.

c   Relation Between Unanimity and Fundamental Comparisons

It is very important to note that unanimous comparisons imply fundamental comparisons. We already have noted this for equivalence, but there also is the following property.

Theorem
Unanimous preference implies fundamental dominance.

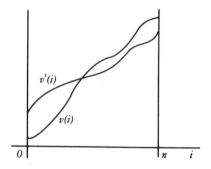

Figure 34

An immediate corollary is that unanimous preference or equivalence implies fundamental dominance or equivalence. On the whole,

$$Z(UE)Z' \Rightarrow Z(FE)Z'$$

$$Z(UP)Z' \Rightarrow Z(FD)Z'$$

$$Z(UPE)Z' \Rightarrow Z(FDE)Z'.$$

To prove the theorem, it is sufficient to prove it when Z and Z' differ only by one of their elements z_i. Indeed, we can pass from a Z' to a Z which is unanimously preferred to it by a succession of modifications of one element at a time. The property of transitivity then proves the theorem in the general case.

Let Z and Z' be such that $z_j = z'_j$ for all $j \neq i$ and $z_i \succ z'_i$. The essence of the proof is that when z'_i is transformed into z_i it passes from the rank k' in the sequence of the ζ'_j to the rank $k \geq k'$ in the sequence of the ζ_j, and that thus all the ζ'_j for $j < k'$ and $j > k$ remain unchanged, whereas those for j between k' and k would have a rank one unit lower in the sequence of the ζ_j and thus improve, or at least do not worsen, the level in their new rank. Precisely, k' and k are such that

$$\zeta'_{k'} = z'_i$$

$$\zeta_k = z_i,$$

and we have $k \geq k'$. Then,

$$\zeta_j = \zeta_j' \qquad \text{for all } j < k' \text{ and } j > k,$$

$$\zeta_j = \zeta_{j+1}' \succsim \zeta_j' \qquad \text{for } k' \leq j < k,$$

$$\zeta_k \succsim \zeta_{k-1} = \zeta_k'.$$

This shows that $Z_0(UP)Z_0'$, and thus $Z(FD)Z'$.

Moreover, if $z_i \sim z_i'$ and $z_j = z_j'$ for all $j \neq i$, then $Z_0(UE)Z_0'$, and $Z(FE)Z'$.

The proof also shows that $z_i \succ z_i'$ for all i implies $\zeta_i \succ \zeta_i'$ for all i.

This theorem implies the three following characteristic properties of fundamental dominance, each of which can define fundamental dominance.

Corollaries
Three conditions necessary and sufficient for one state to fundamentally dominate another are:

1. *One of its permuted states is unanimously preferred to a permuted state of the other state;*

2. *The state is unanimously preferred to a permuted state of the other state;*

3. *One of its permuted states is unanimously preferred to the other state.*

If condition 1 is sufficient, conditions 2 and 3 also are, since identity is a particular permutation. Condition 1 is necessary since it suffices to take the ordered states as permuted states. Condition 1 is sufficient since, according to the theorem, this permuted state fundamentally dominates the permuted state of the other, and hence its ordered state is unanimously preferred to the ordered state of the permuted state of the other, which shows that the state fundamentally dominates the other state since we can take the same ordered state for a state and for its permuted states. Finally, the necessity of conditions 2 and 3 is readily seen since, if $Z(FD)Z'$, then $Z_0(UP)Z'_0$, that is, calling π and π' ordering permutations,

$$\pi Z(UP)\pi'Z',$$

hence

$$Z(UP)\pi^{-1}\pi'Z'$$

and

$$\pi'^{-1}\pi Z(UP)Z'.$$

Taking account of the analogous properties for fundamental equivalence found above, similar properties for fundamental dominance or equivalence obtain. Corresponding properties for the relation $\zeta_i \succ \zeta'_i$ for all i can also be derived.

d Counting Comparisons

The *number classification function* of a social state $Z = \{z_i\}$ is a function from the generic z to the set of integers, defined as: $N(z)$ is the number of elements z_i in Z such that $z_i \precsim z$.

Given two social states Z and Z' with number classification functions $N(z)$ and $N'(z)$, say that:

Z and Z' are countably equivalent, noted $Z(CE)Z'$, when $N(z) = N'(z)$ for all z;

Z countably dominates Z', noted $Z(CD)Z'$, when $N(z) \leq N'(z)$ for all z, and $N(z) < N'(z)$ for at least one z;

Z countably dominates Z' or is countably equivalent to it, noted $Z(CDE)Z'$, when $N(z) \leq N'(z)$ for all z, that is, $Z(CE)Z'$ or $Z(CD)Z'$.

One can then easily show that these counting relations are equivalent to the fundamental relations, that is, the relations FE and CE, FD and CD, and FDE and CDE, are, respectively, equivalent.

Hence, there are three different but equivalent characterizations of the fundamental dominance or equivalence relations: (1) the existence of permutations leading to the unanimous comparisons, (2) the unanimous comparisons of ordered states, and (3) the counting comparisons.

e Fundamental Efficiency

Since the ordering relations of fundamental dominance generally are not complete, our interest in them is not, in general, that they completely solve the problem by determining the optimum, but that they reduce the set of possible states in which the optimum can be found to the maximal elements of this ordering.

A maximal state for the ordering relation of fundamental dominance, that is, *a possible state that no other possible state fundamentally dominates*, is called a *fundamentally efficient state*; Z is fundamentally efficient if $Z \in P$ and if there is no $Z' \in P$ such that $Z'(FD)Z$.

The relation obtained above between unanimity and fundamental dominance leads to the following results.

Theorem
A fundamentally efficient state is efficient.

Indeed, if a possible state is not efficient, there exists another possible state that is unanimously preferred to it, and thus that fundamentally dominates it, and the first state is consequently not fundamentally efficient.

Thus, *fundamental efficiency implies efficiency*, and *the set of fundamentally efficient states is included in the set of efficient states*. More precisely, we have the following property.

Property
A fundamentally efficient state is an efficient state of which no permuted state is Pareto-dominated by a possible state, or that is Pareto-dominated by no permuted state of a possible state. If all states Pareto-dominated by a possible state are possible in a given problem, the fundamentally efficient states are the efficient states whose permuted states are impossible or efficient.

Indeed, if a state has a permuted state that is possible but inefficient, there exists a possible state that is unani-

mously preferred to this permuted state, and thus this new
state fundamentally dominates the first state which, consequently, is not fundamentally efficient.

In designating a set of fundamentally efficient states
which is included in the set of efficient states, fundamental
dominance reduces the set of states of society among which
we must search for the optimum. And if a possible state is
not fundamentally efficient, one of its permuted states is
Pareto-dominated by a possible state, and hence this
permuted state is possible and inefficient.

This reduction can, a priori, be substantial. For example, figure 35 shows a case with $n = 2$. We see there the
domain $\mathcal{P}$ of possible U, and the bisector of the axes which
is the locus of the U of just states. The line AB, belonging
to the border of $\mathcal{P}$, is the locus of the U of efficient states.
AB and the first bisector of the axes intersect at J. The
locus of the U of fundamentally efficient states is only the

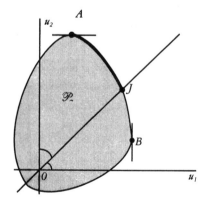

Figure 35

AJ portion of *AB*.[8] The efficient states are those with their *U* on *AB*, the fundamentally efficient states are those with their *U* on *AJ*.

It is even possible that the criterion of fundamental efficiency suffices to solve the problem of determining the optimum, if the domain of possible states has the right structure. Thus, in a case with $n = 2$, figure 36 shows a situation in which $\mathcal{P}$ is such that all the fundamentally efficient states are unanimously equivalent. These states are all the possible states with their *U* being *A*. Note that in this situation efficiency alone does not solve the problem

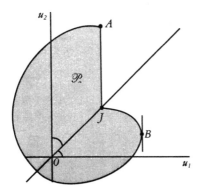

Figure 36

---

8. *Translator's note*: Note that permutations of the states represented by points in *JB*, represented by points of the reflection of *JB*, are dominated by states represented by points in *AJ*.

because the efficient states consist of the possible states whose U is A or is on the JB line, and they are not unanimously equivalent to one another. The optimum is even uniquely defined if there is only one possible state whose U is A.

If the possibility domain $\mathcal{P}$ is bounded toward higher u_i, which certainly is the case, there always exist fundamentally efficient states (the required closedness can always be assumed for practical purposes). Furthermore, if we define a measure on the set of efficient states, the proportion, suitably defined, of fundamentally efficient states within efficient states *prima facie* and in general decreases rapidly as n increases. Indeed, a given efficient state has $n!$ permuted states, and for it to be fundamentally efficient all the other $n! - 1$ must be undominated by possible states, an occurrence which is less likely to be true when the number of different individuals is larger. Only full symmetries in $\mathcal{P}$ would restrict this restriction. But when we conceptually build fundamental utility by transferring into the variables given parameters of the utility functions which describe or cause eudemonistic or satisfaction capacities and which are different for different individuals, we *ipso facto* introduce dissymmetries (non-permutabilities) in the set P, and, roughly speaking, dissymmetrization of P withdraws the status of fundamental efficiency from most efficient states for which all permuted states were efficient.

f The Case of Just States

The properties studied above lead to noteworthy conclusions when just states are considered. We will identify them before briefly stating their reason.

Properties

1. *If one of the two states compared is just, the unanimous and fundamental relations are identical.* More precisely, if Z or Z' is just,

$$Z(UP)Z' \Leftrightarrow Z(FD)Z'$$

$$Z(UE)Z' \Leftrightarrow Z(FE)Z'.$$

2. *A state fundamentally equivalent to a just state is itself a just state that is unanimously equivalent to the first state.*
3. *All just and efficient states are fundamentally and unanimously equivalent to one another.*
4. *A just and efficient state is fundamentally efficient.*

These properties are easily shown, and hence we will only outline their proofs.

For the first properties, since unanimous relations imply fundamental relations, it is sufficient to prove the converse.

Thus, if $Z(FD)Z'$, and if Z' is just, this fundamental dominance implies that Z is unanimously preferred to some permuted state of Z'. But this permuted state is also just and it is unanimously equivalent to Z'. Hence, $Z(UP)Z'$.

Similarly, if $Z(FD)Z'$, and if Z is just, this fundamental dominance implies that there is a permuted state of Z that is unanimously preferred to Z'. But this permuted state also is just and is unanimously equivalent to Z. Hence $Z(UP)Z'$.

And, if $Z(FE)Z'$ where Z or Z' is just, this means that there exists a permuted state of this state which is unanimously equivalent to the other. But this permuted state also is just and is unanimously equivalent to this state. Hence $Z(UE)Z'$.

On the other hand, if there were two just and efficient states not fundamentally and unanimously equivalent to one another, their respective z_i would be in different equivalence classes of fundamental preference, and one would be unanimously preferred to the other. Hence, since the former state is possible, the latter could not be efficient, a contradiction.

Finally, if a just state is not fundamentally efficient, there exists a possible state that is unanimously preferred to one of this just state's permuted states, and hence to this just state itself, and this just state is not efficient. Thus, if a state is just and efficient, it also is fundamentally efficient.

g Structure of a Social Utility Function

If there exists a social utility function representing "social preferences" on states of society, the properties studied above correspond to structures of this function. Let $S(Z) = S(z_1, z_2, ..., z_n)$ be this function, and continue the convention that mentioning u_i implies assuming the existence of the index u.

Unanimous equivalence is equivalent to S depending on Z only through the intermediary of the u_i, that is, to the existence of a function M of the u_i such that

$$S(Z) \equiv M(u_1, u_2, ..., u_n).$$

Unanimous preference is equivalent to the existence of such a function M which is, furthermore, an *increasing function* of each of its arguments.

Permutation equivalence is equivalent to symmetry of S in the set of the z_i, and thus, if furthermore one of the two preceding properties holds, it is equivalent to the existence of such a function M which is a *symmetric function* of the set of its arguments u_i.

Fundamental equivalence is, therefore, equivalent to the existence of a *symmetric function* $M(u_1, u_2, ..., u_n)$.

Fundamental preference is equivalent to the existence of an *increasing symmetric function* of its arguments $M(u_1, u_2, ..., u_n)$.

The states that render $M(u_1, u_2, ..., u_n)$ maximum in the domain of possible states are efficient if M is an *increasing function* of its arguments and they are *fundamentally efficient* if M is an *increasing and symmetric function* of its arguments.

h A Relation Among Fundamental Dominance, Equity, and Adequacy

We have seen that equitable and adequate states, when they exist, are those where an increasing and symmetric function of the set of the n u_i takes its maximum value in the set of states derived from one another by reassignments of the n x_j to the n y_i. We have also seen that this also holds for "restricted" R-equity or R-adequacy, that is, equity and adequacy restricted to any given subset R of these assignments, and for the maximum value of this function in this subset (R is the set of possible assignments for the corresponding realistic equity or adequacy, and general equity and adequacy correspond to the case where R is the set of the $n!$ assignments of the x_j to the y_i)—cf. section III.B.2. Thus, the remarks of the previous section show that R-equitable and R-adequate assignments, when they exist, are the assignments of R that fundamentally dominate or are equivalent to all assignments in R. This can also be shown directly, and the fact that the relations between equity and adequacy were proved in using any increasing and symmetric function M suggests that it can be shown in using the relation of fundamental dominance or equivalence.

Indeed, consider one assignment denoted as $Z = \{z_i\}$ with $z_i = (x_i, y_i)$. Denote as π a n-permutation from i into $\pi(i)$ for each i. Let R denote a set of assignments of the x_j to the y_i, and P_R denote the set of the corresponding permutations, with $Z \in R$ and $1 \in P_R$ (1 denotes the unit or invariant permutation).

If Z is R-equitable,

$(x_i, y_i) \succsim (x_{\pi(i)}, y_i)$ for all i and all $\pi \in P_R$,

that is, $Z(UPE)Z'$ for all $Z' = \{(x_{\pi(i)}, y_i)\} \in R$, which implies $Z(FDE)Z'$ for all $Z' \in R$.

If Z is R-adequate,

$(x_i, y_i) \succsim (x_i, y_{\pi^{-1}(i)})$ for all i and all $\pi \in P_R$,

and hence $Z(UPE)Z''$ where $Z'' = \{(x_i, y_{\pi^{-1}(i)})\}$. But $Z''(PE)Z'$ where $Z' = \{(x_{\pi(i)}, y_i)\}$ and PE denotes permutation equivalence. Hence $Z''(FE)Z'$. Therefore $Z(FDE)Z'$ for all $Z' \in R$.

There results that no $Z' \in R$ can fundamentally dominate a R-equitable or a R-adequate state $Z \in R$.

This also provides another proof of the relation between equity and adequacy, and R-equity and R-adequacy, presented in section III.B.2. Indeed, both all R-equitable assignments, and R-adequate assignments, when they exist, coincide with the maximal elements of the partial ordering *PRE* of R. Hence if R contains both R-equitable and R-adequate assignments, their sets coincide and each state that has one property also has the other.

Property
When they exist, R-equitable and R-adequate assignments are the maximal elements of the relation of fundamental preference or equivalence in R. Hence, if both properties are possible, each state that has one has the other. This holds in particular for general equity and adequacy.

5 Practical Justice

a Definition and Logic of Practical Justice

There may exist no efficient just state, or even no possible just state: Justice can be inefficient, and thus doubtless non-optimal, or even simply impossible. One can then take advice from Kant: when a categorical imperative is not possible, follow the closest pragmatic imperative. The concepts analyzed heretofore—efficiency (and thus unanimity), equity, adequacy, fundamental efficiency (and thus fundamental dominance)—do not, in general, solve the problem of determining the optimum, because they do not designate a unique state. To resolve the problem in general, it is necessary to find a more powerful criterion, that is, a more selective criterion. It would be sufficient, for example, to have a complete ordering.

I have proposed such an ordering, and the criterion derived from it, called *practical justice*. Its ethical value can be very strong, although, as we will see, it is not universal. When justice defined above can be efficient, practical justice reduces to it in the sense that it designates the just and efficient state (or any one among them) as the optimum. The adjective "practical" is here for its Kantian meaning of taking account of the requirement and constraints of reality (a concept of "second best").

The idea of practical justice is the following. The consideration of fundamental preferences allows us to compare and to classify the "happiness" of different individuals. The proposition is, then, to begin with taking care of the most unfortunate or unhappy. If her lot improves in such a way that she ceases to be the most unhappy person, then we concern ourselves with the new most unhappy. And so on. But, with the most unhappy person being as happy as possible, there can be several possible levels of happiness for the other persons. The criterion should therefore be completed. This is done in the obvious manner: Given that the least happy persons (there may be several) are as happy as possible, first minimize their number, and second, continue to apply the criterion to the other persons. Thus, given the level of happiness and the number of least happy persons, the individuals in the second level of increasing happiness will be made as happy as possible. This continues until the most fortunate members of the society are made as happy as possible, given that the others already have been made as happy as possible with the described order of priority. The final state will be called *practically just*.

Choosing in this manner between only two states yields the announced binary relation. This choice is made in the following way. The least happy individuals in each of the two states are compared, and the state in which they are happier is chosen. Of course, these individuals are not in general the same in the two states. If they happen to be equally happy but not in the same number in the two states, the state in which they are the least numerous is chosen. If they are both equally happy and in the same number in the two states, then the individuals at the next level of happiness are compared, and the state in which they are happier is chosen. If these individuals are equally happy, we continue in the same manner. The state thus chosen is said to be *practically more just than the other*. It is clear that the only case in which one cannot so choose is that in which these two states are fundamentally equivalent.

Let us illustrate these concepts.

If $n = 2$, the criterion requires that the smaller of the two numbers, u_1 and u_2, is made as large as possible. This is the "maximin" criterion

$$\underset{Z \in P}{\text{Max}} \quad \text{Min} \ \{u_1, u_2\}.$$

Figure 37 shows the space of the U in cases that differ with respect to the form of the domain of possible states and it shows $\mathcal{P}$, the space of the possible U. In figure 37(a) there exist just and efficient states (at least one) for which the U is J: clearly it is the choice to which the described criterion leads. In figure 37(b), on the other hand, a just and efficient state does not exist, and we see that a practically just state has for its U the point Ω, in which the smaller of the u_i ($i = 1, 2$) is as large as possible.

For any n, the states are entirely judged by their curve of ordered utilities. If two states have different v_1, the state with the higher one is "practically more just" than the other. Otherwise, these states are compared exclusively by the first of the v_i in which their curves of ordered utilities separate from one another. The state for which this v_i is higher is "practically more just" than the other: in figure 38, Z is "practically more just" than Z'.

This criterion of practical justice that we saw to be a "maximin" for $n = 2$, can, in the general case, be called by extension a *lexicographic maximin*, or *leximin*, the order of the lexicography being the order of increasing happiness.

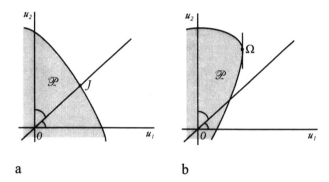

Figure 37

Hence practical justice is leximin with fundamental preferences, or *fundamental leximin*.

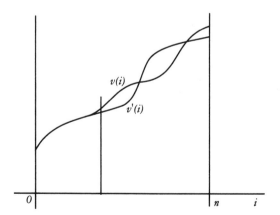

Figure 38

Now we will give more precise definitions. Write $Z(PJ)Z'$ for "Z is practically more just than Z'." By definition, $Z(PJ)Z'$ means that there exists one i, $1 \le i \le n$, such that $\zeta_i \succ \zeta_i'$ and $\zeta_j \sim \zeta_j'$ for all $j < i$ if $i > 1$ (hence $1 \le j < n$). We easily see that this relation has the following properties.

It is *transitive*:

$$Z(PJ)Z' \text{ and } Z'(PJ)Z'' \Rightarrow Z(PJ)Z''.$$

It is *antisymmetric*:

$$Z(PJ)Z' \text{ excludes } Z'(PJ)Z.$$

It thus constitutes a *strict ordering* of the Z.

We easily see that for any pair of states Z and Z', one and only one of the three following relations is satisfied: $Z(PJ)Z'$, $Z'(PJ)Z$ or $Z(FE)Z'$.

Practical justice and fundamental equivalence satisfy the following "laws of composition":

$$Z(PJ)Z' \text{ and } Z'(FE)Z'' \Rightarrow Z(PJ)Z''$$

$$Z(FE)Z' \text{ and } Z'(PJ)Z'' \Rightarrow Z(PJ)Z''.$$

Define

$$Z(PJE)Z' \Leftrightarrow Z(PJ)Z' \text{ or } Z(FE)Z'.$$

This new relation is transitive. It thus is an *ordering* relation. Its "laws of composition" with fundamental equivalence and practical justice are obvious. Fundamental equivalence and the relation of practical justice are, respectively, the relations of equivalence and of strict ordering associated with this relation. But what is particularly noteworthy is that the relation *PJE* is *complete*: Given any pair of states Z and Z', we have

$$Z(PJE)Z' \text{ or } Z'(PJE)Z,$$

with the possibility of having both at the same time, in which case, moreover, $Z(FE)Z'$.

It follows from this that the maximal elements of the relation of practical justice on the domain of possible states, P, are on the one hand fundamentally equivalent to one another, and on the other hand such that each is practically more just than all the other possible states. Consequently, the concept of practical justice *solves the problem posed*.[9] One such state will be said to be *practically just*, and, denoting it Z_j, it is defined by: $Z_j \in P$, and there does not exist $Z \in P$ such that $Z(PJ)Z_j$. We also have the property that any state fundamentally equivalent to a practically just state is practically just. These states thus constitute a fundamental equivalence class.

In summary, *a practically just state is a possible state practically more just than all the possible states that are not practically just,* and *all practically just states are*

---

9. With the required closure of the possibility set: see the next section.

fundamentally equivalent to one another and constitute a fundamental equivalence class. Of course, there may be only one practically just state, and certainly this is the common case.

We see straightforwardly that *fundamental dominance implies practical justice*, that is,

$$Z(FD)Z' \Rightarrow Z(PJ)Z'.$$

It follows that *unanimity implies practical justice* in the sense of

$$Z(UP)Z' \Rightarrow Z(PJ)Z'.$$

Consequently, no possible state can fundamentally dominate a practically just state or be unanimously preferred to it. That is, *a practically just state is efficient*, and, even, *a practically just state is fundamentally efficient.*

The converse relations between practical justice on the one hand, and fundamental dominance and unanimous preference on the other, in general do not hold. The exception is when the "inferior" state is just. Indeed, we see immediately that if Z' is just,

$$Z(PJ)Z' \Rightarrow Z(FD)Z'.$$

Consequently, in taking account of the preceding results, if Z' is just,

$$Z(PJ)Z' \Leftrightarrow Z(FD)Z' \Leftrightarrow Z(UP)Z':$$

if the "inferior" state is just, then practical justice, funda-mental dominance and unanimous preference are identical relations.

The relations among justice, efficiency and practical justice derive from this. Let Z be an efficient and just state. If there were a possible state Z' such that $Z'(PJ)Z$, we would have $Z'(UP)Z$ since Z is just. But, this is impossible since Z is efficient. Thus, there exist no such Z', that is, Z is practically just. Practically just states then are the possible states fundamentally equivalent to Z, but this fundamental equivalence is identical to unanimous equiva-lence since Z is just. We thus have the following proper-ties:

- *A just and efficient state is practically just.*
- *If there exists a just and efficient state, the practically just states are the possible states that are unanimously equivalent to that state.*

Finally, note that, because of its lexicographical charac-ter, the ordering relation of practical justice is not in general representable by a "social utility function." Howev-er, if, given that u exists, all the states considered have different v_1, the social utility function exists and it is Min u_i or any increasing function of this value which is also v_1.

b Ethical Value and Limit of Practical Justice

Practical justice is an extremely satisfying concept from certain points of view: it recommends first to take care of those who are most unhappy, and it solves the logical problem of determining the optimum. But it is essential to see its ethical meaning. To give priority to the least happy can be related to egalitarian aspirations (at least it yields equality if equality is efficient). However, it is not egalitarian to the point of wishing to achieve some equalization of happinesses by reducing that of the happiest when other things, and in particular the happiness of the least happy, are given. In summary, *practical justice can be seen as the most egalitarian recommendation possible that is compatible with efficiency*. One could say that it is intelligent radicalism. But there also are limits to the ethical value of this concept.

Assume, for example, two states A and B such that millions of individuals are happier in A than in B, and only one individual is happier in B than in A; but that in each of the two states this individual is less happy than all the others, according to fundamental preferences. Practical justice leads to preferring state B to state A. It puts all the weight on the least happy individual and takes account solely of her situation to the exclusion of all others. One can find this good, but one also can deplore that the happiness of millions is sacrificed for the happiness of only one, however unhappy he may be. And he may not be unhappy, or much less happy than others, or the others may be much happier in A than in B while the least happy individual is almost indifferent between these two states (these expressions introduce more structure in preferences than the unique orderings considered so far). Could one jeopardize the well-being of millions of individuals in order to elicit a faint smile on the face of the congenitally saddest one? There can be "maximin exploitation" by the least happy. This criticism is not significantly weakened when we consider that the most unhappy individuals in *A* and *B* can be different. Furthermore, as we have noted, in a number of problems and situations, satisfaction or happiness is not the relevant end value of justice.

Finally, practical justice is the relevant principle when the least happy are particularly miserable, in cases of deep suffering or non-satisfaction of basic needs, and when the improvement of these situations is not too costly for people who are not very much better off. Note that it is then usually rather clear who the most miserable are. This constitutes *conditional practical justice*. In addition, practical justice can and often should be used in *association* with other criteria. Since it is a practically complete principle, the others can stand as side constraints. One then has *restricted practical justice*. Societies give such a position to the respect of a number of rights whose extent characterizes the social and economic system. In a full market system, practical justice can be restricted to the primary allocation of nonhuman natural resources. The minimal set of rights shared by liberal-democratic regimes are the basic rights of man and of the citizen, and they can constitute the side constraints of the eudemonistic fundamental leximin of practical justice. The optimal, and hence possible, set of liberal side constraints will depend on a number of aspects of the society, and notably its affluence, and its integration and sense of community and solidarity.

6 Questions of Existence

One very important problem has not yet been raised in this chapter, that of the existence of states endowed with the properties under consideration: do there exist efficient, fundamentally efficient, or practically just states? The reason the answer to this question was not studied as each concept was presented is that it reduces to discussion of a property that is of no economic interest—it thus presents the curious feature of being both very important, and yet of very little interest. This property is the *closure* (in the topological sense) of the set of possible states for the ordering relations being considered. It also reduces to questions of closure of the domain $\mathcal{P}$ of the space of U at certain points on its border. If the number of possible Z is finite, all the required properties of closure are satisfied, and there exists at least one efficient state, at least one fundamentally efficient state, and at least one practically just state (in fact, the last property implies the other two and the second implies the first). However, if this number is infinite, and, in particular, if the infinity is not denumerable, it is necessary to add hypotheses of closure to ensure these existences. It really is not restrictive to make these assumptions because, practically—and provided that we have a function u bounded on the set of z encountered when Z describes P (which is not restrictive either)—, the presence or absence of closure amounts to distinguishing among states infinitely close to one another that individuals are not sufficiently sensitive to discern.

It suffices to consider the broadest hypothesis, that is, the closure of the set P under the relation of unanimous preference. It is identical to the closure of $\mathcal{P}$ on the side of the U of efficient states. This hypothesis also amounts to saying that for any possible and non-efficient state there exists at least one efficient state that is unanimously preferred to it. As a result of this hypothesis, if P is not empty, that is, if there exists at least one possible state, then there exists at least one efficient state, at least one fundamentally efficient state, and at least one practically just state (the last property implying the other two, and the second implying the first).

Then, the following further properties hold:

Theorem
If all the efficient states are fundamentally equivalent, they are fundamentally efficient.

Corollary 1
If all the efficient states are unanimously equivalent, they are fundamentally efficient.

Corollary 2
If there is a single efficient state, it is fundamentally efficient.

Since unanimously equivalent states also are fundamentally equivalent, the corollaries follow immediately from the theorem.

The theorem is proved as follows. Let Z be an efficient state. If it were not fundamentally efficient, there would exist a possible state Z' such that $Z'(FD)Z$. This Z' cannot

be an efficient state since by hypothesis all the efficient
states are fundamentally equivalent to Z, which precludes
this fundamental dominance. There thus exists an efficient
state Z'' such that $Z''(UP)Z'$. But since Z'' is efficient,
$Z''(FE)Z$. Now $Z''(UP)Z'$ implies $Z''(FD)Z'$ which, with
$Z'(FD)Z$, implies $Z''(FD)Z$. And these two relations
between Z'' and Z are contradictory. Z therefore is fundamentally efficient.

7 Fundamental and Extremal Majorities, Fundamental Rank Principles

What else can we do when we restrict ourselves to individual preferences that exclusively rank pairs of states? One
possibility is to count the individuals who have such a
preference. This is what the criterion of unanimity does.
It is also what is involved in the most frequently used
procedure of collective choice, majority voting. The criti-
cisms addressed to this are well known. One is the failure
to take into account "intensities of preferences," but it is
precisely for this reason that it requires only rankings of
states. The other is that comparison by pairs utilizing the
method of majority voting is generally an intransitive
relation (the "Condorcet paradox"). This intransitivity,
however, is not actually a serious problem, since a voting
procedure does not consist of an unstructured set of votes
between pairs, but has other structure, organization and
rules that lead to the choice (the possibility of intransitivity
disturbs only people who believe in an anthropomorphic
maximizing "general will"). Yet there are several types of
majority voting and to choose one of them implies an

ethical choice (for example, comparison between pairs at strict majority, or two-thirds majority or some other fraction, or choosing among more than two states at relative majority).   For pairwise comparisons only unanimity (100%) appears to be an "objective" number, a priori, although next to it the 50% majority (which is both "absolute" and "relative") also seems to possess a certain "a priori objectivity" when the practical choice involved is not specified.[10]

Consideration of fundamental preferences gives a new richness to all criteria. Thus, introduced into the unanimity criterion it gave fundamental dominance. More generally, it should be associated with the majority criteria. It should in particular be associated with the most common majority criterion, the pairwise comparison of alternatives using a one half majority, i.e., the criterion ordinarily meant by the term "majority" without qualification. We will thus have the following definitions.

Z wins by majority over Z' if there are more i such that $z_i \succ z'_i$, than i such that $z'_i \succ z_i$.

Z wins by *fundamental majority* over Z' if there are more i such that $\zeta_i \succ \zeta'_i$, than there are i such that $\zeta'_i \succ \zeta_i$. In considering the curves of ordered utilities $v(i)$ and $v'(i)$ (figure 39), Z wins by fundamental majority over Z' if the

---

10. See also, in section 4.d. of "The Optimal Production of Social Justice" (op. cit.), the special significance and importance of "approximate unanimity" and "recurrent quasi-unanimity," i.e., successive small moves each wanted by $n - 1$ individuals where n is the total number of individuals.

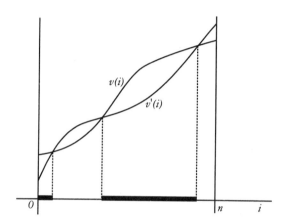

Figure 39

total length on the i axis where $v(i)$ is above $v'(i)$ exceeds
the total length where $v(i)$ is below $v'(i)$.

Obviously, if $Z(UP)Z'$, Z wins by majority over Z'.
And thus any possible state such that no other possible state
wins over it by majority is efficient (if it were not efficient,
another possible state would win over it by Pareto-
unanimity, and hence by majority).

Similarly, if $Z(FD)Z'$, Z wins by fundamental majority
over Z'. And, consequently, if $Z(UP)Z'$, then Z wins by
fundamental majority over Z' since $Z(UP)Z' \Rightarrow Z(FD)Z'$.
Thus, *any possible state such that no other possible state
wins over it by fundamental majority is fundamentally
efficient* (and thus efficient). Indeed, if Z is not fundamentally efficient, there exists a possible state Z' such that
$Z'(FD)Z$, and Z' wins over Z by fundamental majority.

In this way, majority and fundamental majority play the desired role of reducing social choice to subsets of the sets of efficient and fundamentally efficient states.

The relation of fundamental majority also generally is intransitive, as can be easily seen. And it, in some sense, falls into the opposite failing as that of practical justice, in giving the same weight in the social choice to all levels of happiness. One can remedy this defect in preferring Z to Z' whenever $\sum_{i=1}^{n}(n + 1 - i) \cdot sgn(v_i - v_i') > 0$, or more generally $\sum_{i=1}^{n} f(i) \cdot sgn(v_i - v_i') > 0$ where $f(i)$ is a nonincreasing function, which includes, as particular cases, fundamental majority when f is constant, the preceding case when f is linear, max min$_i$ u_i when $f(1) > 0$ and $f(i) = 0$ for $i > 1$, and practical justice when f decreases sufficiently rapidly. A convex function f is likely to be suitable. The case $f(i) = 1/i$ is likely to be close to practical justice. The family $f(i) = i^{-\alpha}$ with $\alpha > 0$ permits modulation of the weighting effect, and we will often want $\alpha < 1$. As a general rule, nontransitivity will tend to be the less frequent, the higher the decreasingness of the function $f(i)$. These forms justify the comparison of Z and Z' through their fundamentally ordered states.

Another approach is to consider n-permutations $\pi(i)$ and the numbers $m(Z, Z', \pi) = \sum_i sgn(u_i - u_{\pi(i)}')$. One has $m(Z, Z', \pi) = -m(Z', Z, \pi^{-1})$. Standard majority and fundamental majority consist in preferring Z to Z' whenever $m(Z, Z', \pi) > 0$ for permutations π that are, respectively, the unit or invariant permutation $\pi = 1$, and an ordering permutation of the u_i' when the i are already relabelled so as to order the u_i. Let us then consider $m^+(Z, Z') = \max_\pi m(Z, Z', \pi)$, and $m^-(Z, Z') = \min_\pi m(Z, Z', \pi)$.

One has $m^+(Z,Z') = -m^-(Z',Z)$.   If $Z(FD)Z'$, then $m^+(Z,Z') > 0$, with furthermore $m^+(Z,Z') = n$ if $v_i > v_i'$ for all i (in particular if $v_1 > v_n'$). One can then choose the principle to prefer Z to Z' whenever the following equivalent relations are satisfied

$$m^+(Z,Z') > m^+(Z',Z),$$

$$m^-(Z,Z') > m^-(Z',Z),$$

$$m^+(Z,Z') + m^-(Z,Z') > 0,$$

$$m^+(Z',Z) + m^-(Z',Z) < 0.$$

This symmetrical binary relation will be called the choice at *extremal majority*. Another principle, the choice at *average or cumulated majority*, consists in preferring Z to Z' whenever $\Sigma_\pi m(Z,Z',\pi) > 0$, where the sum is over the $n!$ permutations π.

When the choice is among more than two alternative states, which is the general case, pairwise comparisons among nonchosen states are useless (and they would be excessive requirements). Relative majority and Borda-like schemes can be much generalized in various ways, notably in order to introduce the fundamental (ordinal) interpersonal comparability. Still with n individuals, let $k = 1, \dots N$ be an index of the N alternative states and denote as u_i^k the fundamental utility level of individual i in state k (it would make no difference to consider orderings, and the representation by a utility function is always possible with finite or denumerable sets of states and of individuals). For each state k, the individuals i can be reordered by a n-permutation $\pi^k(i)$. A set of these N n-permutations is denoted by the index Π. There are $(n!)^N$ such sets. One of them is the invariant unit 1, where $\pi^k(i) = i$ for all i and all k. Another is an ordering set of permutations, ω, for which, for each k, π^k is an ordering permutation of the state k: for each k, $v_i^k = u_{\pi^k(i)}^k$, and $i < j$ entails $v_i^k \leq v_j^k$. Denote as $u(k, i, \Pi)$ the value of u_i^k after the reordering of the indices i by the permutation π^k of Π for each k. For instance, $u(k, i, 1)$ is the original u_i^k, and $u(k, i, \omega) = v_i^k$. For given i and Π, denote as $r(k, i, \Pi)$ the rank in decreasing order of $u(k, i, \Pi)$ for the various states k: there are exactly $r(k, i, \Pi) - 1$ states k' such that $u(k', i, \Pi) > u(k, i, \Pi)$.

The *rank principle* consists in choosing a state k that maximizes $\Sigma_i g[r(k, i, \Pi), \Pi]$ where $g(r, \Pi)$ is a *rank valuation function*, a function decreasing in r. For instance, if $g = 0$ for $r > 1$ and $g > 0$ for $r = 1$, the principle is standard *relative majority* for $\Pi = 1$, and it is *fundamental relative majority* for $\Pi = \omega$. The case $g = N - r + 1$ and $\Pi = 1$ is Borda's principle. The same g and $\Pi = \omega$ can be called the *fundamental Borda principle*. Other notable cases are with $g = r^{-\alpha}$ with $\alpha > 0$, and in particular $g = 1/r$ when Π is 1 or ω.

For $\Pi = \omega$, the *decreasing rank principle* consists in choosing a state k that maximizes $\Sigma_i G[r(k, i, \omega), i]$ where the rank valuation function G is decreasing in both r and i. In particular, the *weighted fundamental relative majority* principle obtains with $G = 0$ for $r > 1$, and $G = f(i) > 0$ for $r = 1$, where $f(i)$ is a decreasing function (for example, $n - i + 1$, $i^{-\alpha}$ with $\alpha > 0$, or $1/r$). Other possible forms of the function G are $C - \alpha r - \beta i$ and $r^{-\alpha} i^{-\beta}$, with α, β, and C being positive constants. The same form, but with a function G increasing in the rank r rather than decreasing, would manifest a moral inspiration in the direction of utilitarianism rather than in the direction of practical justice.

Finally, with a rank valuation function $\gamma[r(k, i, \Pi)]$ and denoting $\Gamma(k, \Pi) = \Sigma_i \gamma[r(k, i, \Pi)]$, other solutions consist in choosing a state k that maximizes $\Sigma_\Pi \Gamma(k, \Pi)$, $\max_\Pi \Gamma(k, \Pi)$, and $\min_\Pi \Gamma(k, \Pi)$. These solutions are relative majorities when $\gamma = 0$ for $r > 1$ and $\gamma > 0$ for $r = 1$.

All these concepts rest on individual preferences represented only by an ordering (or an ordinal utility function). But we may sometimes want to say that state 1 is to be preferred to state 2 because one individual prefers state 1 to state 2 more than another prefers state 2 to state 1, and the others are indifferent. This is a particular case of the notion that an individual prefers state 1 to state 2 more than she, or another individual, prefers state 3 to state 4. This concept is sometimes meaningful. This shows that the concept of preference has more structure than just one ordering. Yet this structure does not lead to cardinality, even in economists' sense, because "individual i prefering state 1 to state 2" has no reason to be expressed by the mathematical difference $u_i^1 - u_i^2$. That is, preference remains an ordinal concept but there can be, in addition, pairwise ranking, and possibly ordering, of pairwise preference comparisons, and even more specific structures of these comparisons of preference comparisons (e.g., state 1 is preferred to state 2 "much more" than state 3 is preferred to state 4, etc.). This structure constitutes a generalization of fundamental dominance, since its simplest subcase amounts to it, as the next section will show.

8 Interpersonal Comparisons of Nested Advantages and Disadvantages

Hence, one can sometimes say that a person "suffers" or "profits" more than another from a defined modification of things, or that "one suffers more than another profits from such a modification" (or *vice versa*). If the interpersonal comparison is represented by the fundamental utility, the remaining issue is the comparison of variations of an ordinal index. No new structure is needed when the intervals of these variations are *included* one in the other.

More precisely, consider two individuals 1 and 2, and two states Z and Z'. We thus have four *levels of the fundamental utility index u* to consider: u_1, u_2, u'_1, u'_2. In passing from Z to Z' the utility index of individual 1 passes from u_1 to u'_1 and that of individual 2 passes from u_2 to u'_2. Let us represent the level of u on an axis (figure 40). Call A_1, A_2, A'_1, A'_2 the points for which the coordinate is, respectively, u_1, u_2, u'_1, u'_2. The inclusion relation considered is that of segments (sets of points) $A_1 A'_1$ and $A_2 A'_2$.

If $A_1 A'_1 = A_2 A'_2$, that is, if $u_1 = u_2$ and $u'_1 = u'_2$ or else $u_1 = u'_2$ and $u'_1 = u_2$, one can say that the passage from Z to Z' creates variations of "utility" of equal intensity—but in the same direction or in the opposite direction, as the case may be—for both persons: one "gains" or "loses" "as much as" the other, or "loses" "as much as" the other "gains." If $A_2 A'_2 \subset A_1 A'_1$, we can say that the "utility" of individual 1 varies more than that of individual 2 when Z'

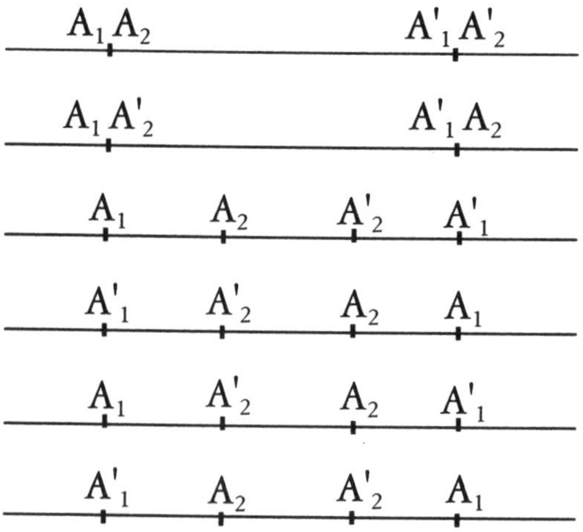

Figure 40

is substituted for Z; if $u_1 < u_2 < u_2' < u_1'$, this change "profits individual 1 more than individual 2"; if $u_1' < u_2' < u_2 < u_1$, individual 1 "suffers more than" individual 2 from the change; if $u_1 < u_2' < u_2 < u_1'$, individual 1 "benefits" more than individual 2 "suffers" from the change; if $u_1' < u_2 < u_2' < u_1$, individual 1 "loses" more than individual 2 "gains." One easily sees how certain of these inequalities can be replaced with equalities while keeping the meaning of these expressions. All these considerations are "ordinal" since they are founded only on the ranking of levels of the fundamental utility index u.

When the utility levels of individuals 1 and 2 vary in the same direction, the unanimity criterion ranks Z and Z'. When they vary in opposite directions and in the cases we have just considered, then to rank Z and Z' according to whether the "advantage" of the substitution to one of the persons is "equal to," "greater than," or "smaller than," its "disadvantage" to the other *amounts to the other case of fundamental equivalence or dominance,* as is easily seen. One also can say that fundamental equivalence and fundamental dominance are generalizations to the case in which there are any number of persons, of the preceding remarks concerning the case in which they are only two.

Obviously, if $A_1 A_1' \subset A_2 A_2'$ the situations are the same, with the indices of the individuals interchanged. But, if there ceases to be a relation of inclusion between the two segments, then, when the individuals have opposite preferences between Z and Z', these comparisons of "intensity" can no longer be made without the introduction of the further structure of the comparison of pairwise preferences noted above.

9   Comparison of Ordinal Inequalities, Inclusion, Truncations

In the ranking of the values u_1, u_2, u_1', u_2' (and hence of the points A_1, A_2, A_1', A_2' on the line), the preceding section concerns the cases where the two extreme values concern the same individual, as do correspondingly the two intermediate values (with possibilities of equalities). In other cases, by contrast, the two extreme values concern the same state, as do correspondingly the two intermediate values (with possibilities of equalities). The former cases correspond, we have noted, to fundamental dominance. The latter cases are no less significant: They mean comparison of inequality of the distribution of the u_i in both states, and we will see that they permit a certain extension of the

comparison to the cases of any number of individuals n.
We will consider a fundamental ordinal utility index, but
the concepts and reasonings apply as well to a fundamental
preference ordering.

When $A_1 A_2 \supset A_1' A_2'$, the distribution of the u_i can
certainly be said to be more equal in state Z' than in state
Z. We will say that it is *inclusion more equal* (or less
unequal). Assume now $n > 2$. We will say that the distribution of the u_i' is inclusion more equal than that of the u_i
if a similar relation holds for all pairs of individuals i, j
whose utility levels are not both constant, and if it holds for
at least one pair. We will furthermore consider that the
pairwise comparisons between equal u_i that change in
remaining equal do not affect the overall inequality.
Finally, the relation "more equal" (or "less unequal") will
be assumed transitive. Then, one can show that the
distribution U' is (inclusion) more equal than the distribution U if and only if there exist two numbers a and b with
$a < b$ such that $u_i \leq a \Rightarrow u_i' = a$, $u_i \geq b \Rightarrow u_i' = b$, and
$a < u_i < b \Rightarrow u_i' = u_i$. This transformation can be called a
truncation, and this U' is a truncation of U (a bitruncation
if $v_1 < a \leq b < v_n$, a lower truncation if $v_1 < a$ while $b \geq v_n$
is not effective, and an upper truncation if $b < v_n$ while
$a \leq v_1$ is not effective). Truncations inclusion-diminish the
inequality of the distribution, and all inclusion-decreases in
inequality are truncations. In a truncation, the lower, or the
higher, or both, parts of the curve of ordered utilities $v(i)$
are replaced by flat horizontal segments. Of course,
permutations of the u_i do not change the inequality of the
distribution of the u_i since the u_i encompass all the relevant
aspects of the individuals for the evaluation of the situation.

Hence successions of truncations and permutations diminish the inequality in the sense considered.

Then, lower inequality may be used to compensate a certain lack of unanimity or of fundamental dominance in the comparison of distributions of the u_i. Lower truncation implies unanimity or fundamental dominance. A *balanced bitruncation* is defined as a bitruncation in which the number of u_i that decrease ($u_i > b$) does not exceed the number of u_i that increase ($u_i < a$). The relation of balanced bitruncation is transitive (and antisymmetric). Social preference for balanced bitruncation constitutes a pairwise comparison stricter than majority or fundamental majority—they imply it—, but which is transitive and constitutes a partial ordering (contrary to the majorities).

Practical justice is implied by preference for balanced bitruncations, and more generally for inclusion-lower inequality (truncation) where v_1 increases. It also is implied by preference for fundamental dominance, in particular, in the case of $n = 2$, in its intrepretation as comparison of interpersonally nested variations in individual utilities.

All the foregoing properties rely only on ordinal utilities.

10 Other Directions

The existence of a cardinal individual utility index, were it so only in the sense that economists usually give to this term (an index defined up to a linear increasing function), would open vast fields of new possibilities to ethical considerations. In particular, we would associate this index with the consequences of fundamental preference. We

would be able then, for example, to apply the ideas of the
second half (sections 6 and 7) of "The Optimal Production
of Social Justice"[11] by taking individual utility indexes
instead of income or wealth.[12] Even utilitarianism would
be a logical possibility since cardinal fundamental utilities
can meaningfully be added, and this would also be the case
of proposals by Nash and Raiffa. Unfortunately, all the
propositions advanced so far to justify cardinal utilities
appear to the author unacceptable either in logic or *for the
ethical usage* that is desired here, be it the consideration of
thresholds of sensitivity (Anderson, Allais), or of risk (von
Neumann, Savage), or of ordinal comparisons of preferences between states taken two at a time.[13] However, certain

---

11. Op. cit.

12. This would amount to attributing the supplementary property of
Shur-convexity to the collective utility function $M(u_1, ..., u_n)$, already
endowed with the properties of being increasing (for unanimity) and
symmetric (for fundamental dominance). This property is identical to the
property that a distribution whose Lorenz Curve is "everywhere above"
that of another is better than that distribution. See also "The Optimal
Production of Social Justice," op. cit. (1966), and *The Foundations of
Public Economics: Introduction to the Theory of the Economic Role of
the State* (I.F.P., Paris, 1964).

13. Consider four states A, B, C, D. It may make sense to say: "I
prefer A to B more than I prefer C to D." Various authors started from
there in a polemic in the years 1945-52, and later in a very mathemati-
cally refined article by Suppes, to "prove" the existence of a cardinal
utility. However, at one point in their reasoning all these authors
introduce the idea that this comparison implies the existence of a utility
index u such that $u(A) - u(B) > u(C) - u(D)$, from which they deduce
that this index is well-defined up to an increasing linear function. This

other concepts are sometimes meaningful and help solve the problem (one of them considers comparisons such as "I prefer A to B more than you prefer B to A," a proto-utilitarianism which, however, cannot generally be written with differences of cardinal utilities). Furthermore, it seems that it would be worthwhile to pursue the study of the logical structures of the phenomenon of happiness. There should be something there to find, and this could be very important.[14]

---

conclusion is erroneous because the statement announced can just as well be expressed, for example, by an index u such that

$$\frac{u(A)}{u(B)} > \frac{u(C)}{u(D)},$$

and one moves from one of these two indexes to the other by a logarithmic or exponential, and hence non-linear, transformation, or even by an index u such that $u(A) - [u(B)]^2 > u(C) - [u(D)]^2$ or any other form that is not transformable into a comparison of differences by a transformation of the function u. If the possibly meaningful comparison of preferences between pairs constitutes an ordering that can be represented by a function, all that can be inferred is the existence of an ordinal function $F(A, B)$ such that the comparison is equivalent to $F(A, B) > F(C, D)$. The unwarranted step is the writing of this relation as the comparison between differences of utilities. At most one can find justification to a form $F(A, B) = \Phi[u(A), u(B)]$ with an ordinal function Φ increasing in its first argument and decreasing in its second argument, but nothing justifies that Φ be a function of $u(A) - u(B)$ (except if $u(A)$ and $u(B)$ are very close to each other so that the function Φ can be replaced by its linear approximation).

14. *Author's note of 1997*: Since this was written, progress in this direction has been made in Kolm, "Psychanalyse et théorie des choix" (Psychoanalysis and Choice Theory), *Social Science Information* 1 (1980), and in the books *Le Bonheur-liberté* (Happiness-Freedom)

Finally, despite all the propositions presented here, the theoretical characterization of the social optimum in all its specifications and details is short of being completed. Yet, we have moved a long way from the position, still customary with most economists, that aside from efficiency, "one cannot say anything!" Equity, realistic equities, minimal equity, justice, practical justice, conditional and restricted practical justice, adequacy, fundamental dominance, fundamental efficiency, fundamental majorities, extremal majorities, rank principles, comparisons of inequalities, etc., constitute a panoply of precise concepts with explicit implications and interrelations which we have at our disposal to judge states of society and to help us make the best choice. Even if they still are not sufficient to solve the entire problem, their advantage is undeniable when compared with the vague ethical notions customarily used to justify social choices.

These concepts remain to be applied to social rules, laws, taxes, transfers, etc. Although already explored,[15]

(Presses Universitaires de France, Paris, 1982), second edition 1994, and *L'Homme pluridimensionnel* (Pluridimensional Man) (Albin Michel, Paris, 1987).

15. The concept of fundamental preference is used, for example, in a series of recent studies about optimal redistribution of income, in particular about optimal progressivity of income tax and optimal distribution of public expenditures attributed to various individuals. *Cf.* James Mirrlees, "An Exploration in the Theory of Optimum Income Taxation," *The Review of Economic Studies* (April 1971); Kenneth J. Arrow, "Equity in Public Expenditure," *The Quarterly Journal of Economics* (August 1971); Eytan Sheshinski, "On the Theory of Optimal Income

the work remains almost entirely to be done, and is not
without difficulties. However, only this part of the task
justifies the most theoretical analysis, since for an economist (paraphrasing the most concerned about justice among
us) the point is less to know the world than to improve it.

Taxation" and "The Optimal Linear Income-Tax," discussion papers 171
and 172 (Harvard Institute of Economic Research, February 1971).
However, these authors bypass full consideration of differences in
individuals' tastes, and they deduce their results from the maximization
of a sum of individual utility indices, which in particular implies the
existence of cardinal utility (or from other forms with the same implica-
tion). The present author has dealt with the same problems and others
of this type with only ordinal personal preferences, in the framework of
the concepts of justice presented in this text (see my *Lectures in Public
Economics*, volume 1, *The State and the Price System* (Editions Dunod,
Paris, 1969) and volume 2, *The Economics of Mass Services* (Editions
Dunod, Paris, 1970)), and "On Some Applications of the Principles of
Justice and of Practical Justice," discussion paper (CEPREMAP, 1970)).

Index